PREFACE.

THE Author, emboldened by a Banking expe- rience of over forty years, offers this little work to the public in the hope that, elementary though it be, it may prove acceptable to many persons of both sexes.

The work has been prepared chiefly for the use of women, a vast proportion of whom are brought up in utter ignorance of money matters in the simplest form, though otherwise they may be highly accomplished.

The subject, it must be allowed, is not a fasci- nating one, but there are periods in the lives of most persons when some knowledge of money matters may be useful and even necessary.

W.C.

CONTENTS.

CHAP. I. - What is Money? - What to do with it - How to open a Bank Account - How to draw Cheques

CHAP. II. - How to Deposit Money at Interest - The Bank Pass Book - The Advantages of a Bank Account

CHAP. III. - London Banks and Banking - Bill of Exchange - Deposits - Scotch and Irish Banks

CHAP. IV. - Investments - What are Securities - Mortgages - The Funds - The National Debt - Stocks and Shares - Dividends, how Payable

CHAP. V. - British Government Funds - The Different Debts - Terminable Annuities - Loans Guaranteed by Government - Dividends, how to Receive them - Automatic Reinvestment of Dividends

CHAP. VI. - Government Annuities, how to Purchase - When Payable - Tables - Insurance Office Annuities - Tables - Indian Government Stocks

CHAP. VII. - Loans to Corporations, &c. - Colonial Government Securities - Inscribed Stocks and Bonds - List of Inscribed Stocks - Bonds and Coupons - Foreign Government Stocks - Caution in Investing - Railways - The Different Stocks and their Relative Values - The Warrants for Interest and Dividends - Indian Railway Stocks - American Railways - Foreign Railways - Banks - As an Investment - Colonial and Foreign Corporation Stocks - Canals and Docks - Gas - Electric Lighting, Telegraph and Telephone - Water Works - Breweries - Industrial Companies - Financial, Land and Investment Companies - Financial Trusts - Insurance Companies - Steamship Companies - Mines

CHAP. VIII. - The Stock Exchange - Brokers and Jobbers - How Business is Done - "Contango" and "Backwardation" - "Bulls" and "Bears" - "Boom" and "Slump" - Settlement - Risk in Keeping Convertible Bonds - Brokers - Traps and Snares - Good Companies and Bad - Advertising Swindles - Gold Mines - A Typical Case - Exploration Companies

CHAP. IX. - Life Insurance - Its Advantages - Mutual and Joint Stock Companies - Choice of Office - Form of Proposal - Examination - Premiums, how Payable - Examples of Advantage - Various Modes of Insuring - Bonuses - How Applied - Endowment Insurance - Non-profitable Policies - Settlement Policies - Endowment of Children - Insurance of Joint Lives - Insurance on Longest of Two Lives - Surrenders - Fire Insurance - Farm Stock - Other Insurances

CHAP. X. - A Building Society, Mode of Doing Business - How to Obtain a Share, and Table of Payments - How to Withdraw, and Table - Borrowers - How to Build a House - Table of Payments - How Profits are made - The Weak Points of Societies Badly Conducted - What Leads to Collapse - Necessity for Choosing Directors of Standing and Character - Necessity for Efficient Audit of Accounts

CHAP. XI. - The Post Office Savings Bank - Mode of Depositing - Opening an Account - Convenience and Precautions - Limit in Amounts - Withdrawal - Payment to

EVERYBODY'S GUIDE TO MONEY MATTERS.

CHAPTER I. EASY STEPS TO MONEY MATTERS.

MONEY is the medium by which we may acquire from others, who are willing to part with them, such things as we may desire. The price of an article is the value set upon it by the possessor, as represented by an expressed sum in money.

The price of some things are arbitrarily fixed by law or custom, such as stamps, professional fees, duties, &c.

The standard of value in this country is gold, and it is as against gold, represented by coins of different denominations, that the value of all commodities is estimated.

The authorised coins of the United Kingdom consist of the following pieces:-

GOLD.
Five-sovereign piece, equal to Five pounds.
Two-sovereign piece, equal to Two pounds.
One-sovereign piece, equal to One pound.
Half-sovereign piece, equal to Half-a-pound.

SILVER.
A crown, or five-shilling piece, equal to one-fourth of a sovereign.
Double-fiorin, or four-shilling piece, equal to one-fifth of a sovereign.
Half-a-crown, or two shillings and sixpence, equal to one-eighth of a sovereign.
Florin, or two-shilling piece, equal to one-tenth of a sovereign.
Shilling piece, equal to one-twentieth of a sovereign.
Sixpenny piece, one-half of a shilling.
Threepenny piece, one-half of a sixpence.

BRONZE.
A penny, equal to one-twelfth of a shilling.
Halfpenny, equal to one-half of a penny.
Farthing, one-fourth of a penny.

In writing or speaking of sums of money the expression takes the form of "pounds, shillings, and pence"; for example, Twenty-one pounds five shillings and nine pence. Sometimes the word "sterling" is added, meaning genuine or standard coin of the realm. In accounts the figures are placed in three parallel columns under the heading of £ s. d. "£" for pounds, "s." for shillings, and "d." for pence, from *Libri, solidi*, and *denarii*, the Latin equivalents for these values.

|| | | | || £ | s. | d. | || 21 | 5 | 9 | || || ||

Another form of money, if it may be so termed, is the Bank note. This is simply a promise to pay, on demand, the amount repre- sented on the note, in gold or some legal tender. The most common in use are £5 notes, but there are others of different denominations, such as £10, £20, £50, £100, &c. Some country banks still issue these notes, but they are by law restricted from issuing beyond a certain amount fixed by the Bank Act of 1844. No new bank can issue notes, and those which have the privi- lege are gradually relinquishing it, so that in course of time there will be only one bank entitled to issue notes, and that is the Bank of England.

The notes of country banks, other than the Bank of England, are not a legal tender; that is, it is not compulsory on anyone to accept them in payment of a debt.

The Bank of England is the oldest joint-stock bank in the country, and although, in its consti- tution, it does not differ materially from other joint-stock banks, yet, being the agent of the British Government in all money matters, and possessing other exclusive privileges, it is looked upon as one of the enduring institutions of the country.* (* See Joint-Stock Banks, p. 68.)

Amongst other privileges it enjoys is the authority to issue promissory notes to a certain extent, representing respectively sums of £5, £10, £20, £50, £100, £200, £500, and £1,000.

These Bank of England notes, as they are termed, are absolutely convertible, that is to say, the bank is legally bound to exchange them for gold at all times when demanded; and a cer- tain amount of gold has always, by law, to be kept in stock for the purpose. Moreover, the tender of Bank of England notes, the same as with gold, in payment of a debt, cannot, in this country, legally be refused. No one, however, can be compelled to give change; that is to say, if you owe a person £4 15s., you are bound in strict law to pay him that exact sum. You cannot offer him a five-pound note and insist upon his giving you 5s. change, though, as a matter of courtesy and convenience, payments are constantly accepted in that form.

It must be obvious that these Bank of Eng- land notes are a great convenience, and even a necessity to the public, as it would be quite impossible to carry on the enormous business of the country if such a cumbersome medium as gold coins was the only legal way of paying debt. Nevertheless, gold coin of proper weight is a legal tender to any amount. Silver is not a legal tender for sums over two pounds, nor bronze for sums over one shilling.

But even with bank-notes the requirements of business are not fully satisfied, as there is always the risk of their being lost or stolen. To avoid this risk, and to provide facilities for buying and selling, with the complications inci- dent thereto, and the passing of money from one hand to another, an intermediary agency is required, and that agency is to be found in the banking companies. In nearly every town, having a pretence to the name, in the United Kingdom, will be found a branch bank of some establishment of more or less repute, and those who are fortunate enough to possess money will do well to take advantage of such an agency for their money matters, having, of course, first ascertained that the standing of the company is such that they may do so with safety and confi- dence.

As a first step we give an example of what is occurring daily in hundreds of cases.

Miss Jane Smith is a lady who has been brought up without the slightest instruction in business matters, indeed has rather plumed her- self on the idea of being quite above such things. Suddenly she finds herself dependent upon others for guidance and advice. She would like to act for herself if she only knew how to do so safely, being of a somewhat suspicious temperament and mistrustful of advice from friends or acquaint- ances. Even the highly respectable lawyer, who has handed her a packet of documents and £500 in cash (a legacy from her uncle), with much sage counsel, she is not quite sure about, for she has imbibed the idea from her youth that lawyers are not always to be trusted.

The packet of documents in the tin box as they came to her is set aside in a safe place for the moment, but the bank-notes and gold are a matter of serious concern to her. She fears to carry them about her person lest she should lose them, or be robbed, and feels sure that if kept in the house they will attract any burglars that may be in the neighbourhood.

The best thing Miss Smith can do is to go to one of the neighbouring banks of repute - say the Blankshire Bank - and ask them to help her out of the difficulty.

She has an interview with the Manager or Cashier, tells her story, and is advised to leave the money at the bank and have an account opened in her name. This course she consents to adopt, and hands over the £500, requesting some acknowledgment that she has done so, in common terms, "something to show for it."

Many banks provide and require their cus- tomers to use "paying-in slips," that is, printed forms specifying the payments made to the bank under the head of cheques, notes, gold, and silver. A form is handed in with each payment, and the initials of the cashier placed against the amount noted on the counterfoil, which is re- tained by the customer.

In addition to this Miss Smith will be pre- sented with what is called a pass-book - a book passing between the bank and herself, now become a customer - in which she will find it stated in the briefest business manner, that the Blankshire Bank is Dr. (debtor) to, or owes, Miss Jane Smith £500. She will be told that portions of this money may be drawn out from time to time as she may need it, but this can only be done by cheques, or forms of request to the bank to pay out the amount desired.* These forms, provided by the bank, are printed, blank spaces being left to be filled up in writing, and they are made up in books of various sizes, each form bearing a penny stamp. The customer pays for the book according to the number of stamps it contains, but no more. Miss Smith buys a cheque-book, and, opening it, finds the following form in print:-

(* The practice with some people of writing cheques on plain paper is discountenanced by bankers, and is to be condemned.)

```
_____- |
No. 10901. | No. 10901. _____ 189 | | | | | _____189 | To the
Blankshire Banking Company, | | | Blanktown. | | | | | _____ | Pay
to  _____   or   bearer  |  |  |  |  |  |  the   sum   of
_____ | | | | | £_____ | £_____
_____                |            |            |            |
_____
```

She then recollects that she has no money to go on with, and asks to have £10 of the £500 she has left in the bank. The cashier offers to fill up the blank spaces in her first cheque, making corresponding entries in the counterfoil, and having done so asks her to sign it at the foot.

It then appears as follows:-

```
——————————————————————————————————————————————————-  |
No. 10901. | No. 10901. __March_I,_ 1898 | | | | | March I, 1898 | To the
Blankshire Banking Company, | | | Blanktown. | | | | | ____Self_____ | Pay to
___Self_____      or   bearer  | | | | | |  the  sum  of
___Ten_Pounds_____ | | | | | £10_____ | £10_____
__Jane_Smith__                |           |            |            |
——————————————————————————————————————————————————-
```

The cheque is detached from the counterfoil at the dotted line, and is retained by the cashier, who hands over £10 to the lady together with the book containing the remaining cheques.

"Oh! I had quite forgotten - I owe Miss Tucker, the milliner, £23 10s. Will the cashier please to let me have £23 10s. to pay her with."

Miss Smith is told that there is no need of incurring the risk of carrying the money through the streets, as a cheque in favour of Miss Tucker will equally answer the purpose; and again he fills up the blank spaces in a second cheque, which appears thus:-

```
——————————————————————————————————————————————————-  |
No. 10902. | No. 10902. ! ! __March_I,_ 1898 | | | ! ! | | March I, 1898 | To
the Blank!hir! Banking Company, | | | !Bla!ktown. | | | ! ! order J.S. | |
_Miss_Tucker_ | Pay to ___Miss_Tucker_____ or ====== | | | ! ! | | | the
sum of _Twenty-three_pounds_10/-_ | | | ! ! | | £23_10/-_____ | £23_10/-
```

_____!   !   __Jane_Smith__ | | | !   ! |

_____-

"You see," says the cashier, "I have struck out the word 'bearer' and substituted the word 'order.' This will oblige Miss Tucker to sign her name on the back of the cheque (technically, to 'endorse it') before it can be paid. Your initials are required to confirm the alteration.* I have also drawn parallel lines across the cheque, which makes it what is termed 'a crossed cheque,' and a crossed cheque cannot be cashed direct, but must be paid into an account at a bank. So you see you will have the signature of Miss Tucker, proving that she has been paid her bill by means of this cheque; and it is obvious that by crossing the cheque, should it be lost and made an improper use of, there would be no difficulty in tracing through whose hands it passed."

(* Banks also issue cheques with the word "order" printed instead of "bearer.")

Miss Smith soon learns that all her trades- men's bills may be paid in the same way, with- out going to the bank to draw the money, and with the advantage that the cheque is not only a proof of payment, but that she has also a record of her accounts in the bank pass-book.

It may here be mentioned that should a banker cash a cheque with a forged *endorsement*, he is not responsible, and the loss falls on the drawer of the cheque.* The crossing of a cheque, how- ever, necessitating its being paid to a bank account, would facilitate the discovery of the culprit. An additional security is given to a crossed cheque if it bears the words "not nego- tiable" written underneath the crossing. This means that it cannot legally be used as a means of payment to a third party. In the event of such a cheque going wrong, the loss would fall upon a bank negotiating it for a customer. The bank could be called upon to make good the amount to the payee.

(* If, however, he pays a cheque with a forged signature he is responsible, as he is supposed to know the handwriting of his own customer.)

It is illegal to post-date a cheque, the reason being that bills of exchange, which are obliga- tions to pay money at a future date, bear a much higher stamp duty than cheques. It would, therefore, be a fraud upon the revenue to make cheques do duty for bills of exchange.

CHAPTER II. THE BANK ACCOUNT.

THE manner in which Miss Smith had left her money on what is termed a current account at the Bank is convenient to herself and profitable to the Blankshire Bank, for they have the use of it free, paying nothing for that use in the way of interest.

She will have other money coming to her in the shape of rents, and the interest on money invested, as represented in those documents in the tin box - all which money can be handed over to the Bank in the same way that the £500 was. There is, however, no reason why she should leave so much lying idle without obtaining any interest upon it. She will reckon up how much she will require for, say, the next six months, for house expenses and personal use, and also how much, on the other hand, she will be paid in rents or interest, and will then find that there will be a sum of; at least, say, £300 over and above all she desires to spend.

If she is wise, she will draw out this sum by cheque from her current account and have it placed on a deposit account. In this case the bank will give her a deposit receipt or interest note, somewhat in this form:-

-- |

No. 23975 26th June, 1897. | | | | Blankshire Bank, Blanktown. | | | | RECEIVED from Miss Jane Smith the sum of Three | | Hundred Pounds, to be accounted for with interest at | | 2.5 per cent per annum, on 14 days' notice of | | withdrawl. | | | | Entered - J. Hill T. Dale, Manager. | | |

(and, written across the receipt "Not transferable")

If the money is at any time wanted in a hurry, banks do not insist upon notice being given to withdraw, but deduct the days of notice from the time the interest note has run. For instance, if the money has been deposited for 184 days, the 14 days of notice will be deducted and interest allowed on 170 days only. These receipts or notes are not transferable, and the repayment of the principal or the interest must be applied for by the owner either personally or by letter.

Money may be deposited in a bank in two names and be repayable to both conjointly, by either separately, or to the survivor of the two. The bank will require a form to be signed by both parties, specifying the manner in which it is desired that the money may be deposited. By giving directions, too, the principal may be retained in the name of one person and the interest paid to another. Some banks adopt the plan of book deposits, that is, the amount paid in is entered in a pass-book, and the interest credited half yearly. This may go on accumu- lating, or it can be drawn out in one sum only, not as in the case of a current account by cheques of various amounts.

Having thus established relations between Miss Smith and her bankers, let us see at the end, say, of a month, the state of her pass-book, premising that in the meantime she has received and paid into the bank some moneys, and also signed and sent cheques to some of her trades- men:-

THE BLANKSHIRE BANK.

BLANKTOWN, Dr. to Miss Jane Smith. of Blanktown. Cr.

1897			£	s.	d.	1897			£	s.	d.
June	24	To Cash ..	500	0	0	June	24	By Self ..	10	0	0
July	8	" Dividend Consols	11	4	6	"	"	" Tucker ..	23	10	0
	23	" Rent from Cook	24	10	0	"	26	" Deposit receipt	300	0	0
	25	" G.W.R. dividend	30	0	0	July	1	" Figges ..	8	3	4
						"	3	" Jones ..	5	10	0
						"	24	" Self ..	10	0	0
		Total £565 14s. 6d.						Total £357 3s. 4d.			

By the entries in the pass-book it will be per- ceived that £565 14s. 6d. has been paid into the bank, as appears on the left-hand page, and that £357 3s. 4d. has been drawn out, as appears on the right-hand page. The balance or difference between the two, amounting to £208 11s. 2d., remains to the credit of Miss Smith.

In this comfortable state of things we will leave Miss Smith, who can now claim to consult her banker in matters of business.

He will be able to offer her facilities in various ways. He will hold for her, in safe custody, any deeds or securities; and whilst she is absent from home will take charge of her plate or valu- ables, free of all expense. If she is travelling about the country he will arrange so that her cheques on the Blankshire Bank may be cashed at any other bank in the kingdom. If she has occasion for it he will send money on her account to some other person's credit at any bank in the kingdom or the civilised world. If she desires to travel abroad, he will obtain a passport for her and provide her with "circular notes," which may be turned into money at any place she is likely to visit.

He will buy and sell stocks, shares, annuities, &c., for her, and collect dividends, interest, coupons, &c., payable anywhere at home or abroad. He will cheerfully advise her on all matters connected with money, and it will be quite the exception if she does not, in all things, find him a safe and prudent counsellor.

As a rule, no charge is made by a bank for keeping an account, provided the balance, that is, the amount of money they hold for the cus- tomer - technically the credit balance - is not persistently small. If it were always under £50 that would be considered small, but if only occa- sionally below that figure, and sometimes above £200 for any time, it would generally be exempt from charge. When a charge is made for keeping an account which is not remunerative or free from trouble, it does not amount to much, and is fairly earned.

If an advance of money is required for a tem- porary purpose, the bank will often lend the money by allowing the account to be overdrawn, that is, the balance in the pass-book will appear as due *to* the bank instead of *from* the bank for the sum required from time to time. This is sometimes convenient when the advance is only required for a short time as avoiding the necessity for disturbing any investment which otherwise would have to be sold. As a rule, however (though exceptions are made where the customer is absolutely to be depended upon), the bank would desire some security to be deposited. This may take the form of a sufficient portion in value of stocks or shares in which the customer has invested, or sometimes the personal guar- antee of one or two responsible persons is accepted. This is quite regular business, and the interest usually charged is fair and reasonable.

CHAPTER III. LONDON BANKS AND BANKING.

THE private banks now doing business in London are few in number. The tendency of late years has been to transform these banks into "Limited Liability" Companies, or to amal- gamate with companies of this character. It looks as though, in course of time, private banks will altogether cease to exist, the joint-stock banks being better adapted to modern require- ments. The private banks do not invite deposit, and interest on accounts is not allowed. They look to the average balance on each account to compensate for the trouble and expense of keeping it, with a considerable margin for profit. They require that not less than a certain fixed sum shall be the minimum balance of a customer's account, but, of course, the larger the balance the better for the banker.

The balance in some cases may be very large where the bank has a wealthy connection, it being a boast with some rich persons that they have never less than £10,000, or even £20,000 at their bankers. The money so left in the banker's hands is lent out, or invested in various ways, and all that he receives in the shape of interest, after paying the expenses of his estab- lishment, is clear profit. In short, the £500 a year which the customer might obtain if he in- vested the £20,000 he leaves at the bank, goes to the banker.

At the head of the joint-stock banks of London is the Bank of England, which, like the private banks, do not take deposits upon which interest is allowed, but rely upon the cash at their dis- posal in their customers' accounts for their profits. In all other respects their mode of transacting business is much the same as that of other joint-stock banks. Accounts may be opened by merchants and traders, and by private individuals of known respectability, and no par- ticular sum is required to be lodged upon open- ing the account. Formerly cheques were not allowed to be drawn for a less sum than £10, but now there is no restriction as to the amount. The profits of the bank are chiefly made by dis- counting bills of exchange, which is done to an enormous extent. A bill of exchange is an in- strument by which a party who is owed money by another party, and accords to him the benefit of delay in payment, for a fixed period, draws on him in a form of order to that effect.

For instance, the firm of Bullion & Co. have sold to John Robinson certain goods, which need not be specified, as the principle applies in all cases, whether it be bankers, merchants, or traders, and for all transactions where one party is indebted to another. The form drawn by Bullion & Co. on John Robinson, which requires to be stamped according to the amount, would be as follows:-

---

Due 1st Nov. | | ———————— | | £500 London, 29th Aug., 1987. | | | |
THREE months after date pay to our order the sum of | | Five Hundred
Pounds for value received. | | | | To Mr. John Robinson, Bullion & Co. | |
Merchant, | | Liverpool. | | |

(Written across: Accepted payable at the Bank of London. J. Robinson.)

The acceptance of the obligation by John Robinson is written across the face of the docu- ment, and he makes it payable, as most bills are for convenience, at a London bank, pre- sumably the London agent of his own bankers at Liverpool. Payment becomes due three months after date, with three days of grace added according to custom. Probably Bullion & Co. would find this £500, if in cash, useful in their business, and supposing the parties to be of good repute, they can readily convert it by discounting this bill at their bankers or at a bill broker, who, deducting a small amount in the shape of discount, will hand over the balance to the firm, or carry it to the credit of his account. It is this discount that constitutes the profit to the banker, and the rate varies according to the value of money, whether it is plentiful or scarce.

The rate of discount is supposed to be regu- lated by the Bank of England, and the "bank rate," which is arbitrarily fixed by the directors, is moved up and down (sometimes for other reasons than the value of money), and is sup- posed to be the rate of discount for bills of the best description. It is found in practice, however, that when there is an abundance of money seek- ing employment, bills are discounted at lower rates.

The Bank of England make purchases and sales of British or Foreign securities, and divi- dends on stocks will be received and placed to account. Exchequer bills, bonds, railway deben- tures, or any other securities may be deposited, and the interest, when payable, will be received and placed to a customer's account free of charge. Cash boxes (contents unknown), plate chests, and deed and security boxes are also received for customers for safety, free of charge, and all other banking facilities conceded, as are given by the Blankshire Bank.

The other joint-stock banks of London trans- act their business in all respects in the same manner as the Bank of England. In addition they invite money on deposit, allowing interest on the same. Sums of money lodged on deposit, and they may be by persons who are not other- wise customers, are not carried to a customer's account, but, as in the case of the Blankshire Bank, are placed on a special form of receipt which is changed for a new one when the in- terest or any part of the principal is withdrawn. The rate of interest allowed by the Blankshire Bank, and by the country banks generally, is a fixed one, but that of the London banks is regulated by the value of money, and fluctuates from time to time, notice being given by adver- tisement in the London newspapers of any change in the rate. Deposits are received by the London bankers "at call," that is, payment may be required on demand; or at an arranged term of notice of repayment. The rate of in- terest on money at call is less than where notice is required, and the longer the period of notice the higher the rate of interest.

In Scotland there are no private banks, and in Ireland only two. The joint-stock banks are numerous, and their mode of business is practi- cally the same as in England, indeed the English system is founded on that practised by the Scotch many years before the joint-stock bank was general in England.

CHAPTER IV. INVESTMENTS.

GOING back to the parcel of securities which Miss Smith received from her lawyer, we will presume that they represent safe investments of various kinds. It will be prudent, however, to ask her banker to examine them to see if any, in his judgment, might be sold with advantage (either on account of doubtful character or ex- ceptionally high price), and the money invested elsewhere. This business the bank will transact for her; and in the matter of investment, in addition to using her own common sense as to the nature of the securities in which she should place her money, she should seek the advice of her banker, and rely very much upon his opinion.

The undertakings in which the public are in- vited to invest their money are so numerous, and the prospects of success so speciously asserted, in good and bad alike, that it is necessary to be extremely cautious in accepting any state- ments of the kind without rigid examination and proof of their being true and genuine. Other- wise the investment or purchase becomes a speculation, and, more than likely, will only end in disaster.

The term "securities" applies both to the concerns in which investments are made and to the deeds and documents which represent the investments. Thus a mortgage or a mortgage deed is a "security." The Government Funds, stocks and shares in all companies, bonds, foreign and otherwise, Corporation Stocks, &c., are all termed "securities." A convertible se- curity is one which may be sold in the open market, there being no restriction upon the persons who may hold it.

We will now endeavour to put before the reader some account of the various "securities" in which the public invest their money accord- ing to individual choice, and which (with the exception of mortgage on real property-land or houses) may be bought and sold in the stock- market through the agency of a banker or broker. Quotations of the market price of these securities may be found in the Stock Exchange list, which is published daily, and can be seen at most bankers' offices. Many of them are also quoted in the daily newspapers.

MORTGAGES.

To invest money upon mortgage is to lend it to a person who has house or landed property, and desires to borrow money at a certain speci- fied rate of interest. The title deeds of the property are deposited with the lender of the money, together with a mortgage deed, which describes, in full detail, the terms which may have been agreed upon.

The interest is usually made payable half- yearly, and in the event of its payment not being kept up, or the lender desiring the return of his money, the principal sum can be called up, the lender giving six months' notice of his intention to do so. If the borrower fails to pay, a process of law has to be instituted, called a foreclosure suit, which, if successful, transfers the absolute ownership of the property into the hands of the lender, so that he can receive the rents as his own, or, if he pleases, sell the property under legal authority. In view of such a contingency the value of the property should considerably exceed the amount of the money advanced, so as not only to cover the principal sum, but also any arrears of interest, together with law costs and expenses. The usual pro- portion of an advance on mortgage is two-thirds of the ascertained value of the property, but there might be circumstances which would war- rant some variation in the proportion.

The mortgage deed should be prepared by the lender's own solicitor, who would see that the property had a good title and use all the pre- cautions necessary in transactions of this kind to guard against fraud and loss; and in many cases a professional valuation of the property would be desirable, as a preliminary, before the advance is entertained at all.

Cases have been known where fraudulent per- sons have borrowed money on mortgages of property conveyed to themselves, but as to which they were trustees only for others. The lenders or mortgagees have, in such cases, no alternative but to give up the deeds and submit to the loss of their money.

Debentures are a form of mortgage applicable to the raising of money by a corporation or joint-stock company.

The company mortgages its property for a certain sum, too large for a single person to advance, so it is divided up into even amounts of, say, £100, the money being secured by de- benture bonds, bearing interest at a fixed rate, and being saleable in the stock markets.

THEFUNDS.

"What are the Funds?" The writer has been asked this question over and over again, though it seems scarcely credible that, in these days, any person of ordinary intelligence should be ignorant of the meaning of the term. Unfor- tunately these things are not usually taught in our schools.

"The Funds," generally speaking, is the term applied to the National Debt of Great Britain, the money borrowed by the Government from the people, chiefly for the purpose of carrying on the great wars at the beginning of the present century. For these loans as much as 5 per cent. has in former years been paid, but at present 2 3/4 is the rate payable on the great bulk of the debt.

The year after the Battle of Waterloo the National Debt amounted to nine hundred mil- lions of money; at the present time it amounts to about five hundred and seventy millions, and is steadily diminishing. This being the case, there is of course no need of further borrowing at present, but the loans outstanding - any por- tion of them - may be bought and sold in the market; that is, any lender may transfer all or any part of his loan to some other person, and as there are, daily, hundreds and thousands of individuals wanting to buy or to sell, there is no difficulty whatever, through the medium of the Stock Exchange, in arranging so that a person can obtain, or dispose of, the exact amount of stock he desires.

The chief method by which the National Debt is reduced is described under the head of Terminable Annuities.

STOCKSANDSHARES.

The stock of an institution or company is a fixed sum forming the capital upon which the concern is carried on, or it is the fixed sum bor- rowed for certain purposes. Any quantity of stock may be purchased, but shares, which represent the capital of a company, can only be purchased in whole numbers.

The nominal or face value of stocks and shares by no means necessarily represents their market value; in fact it is the exception that they should do so. The market price is con- tinually fluctuating. Thus, if the price of a given stock is quoted in the lists and news- papers at 110, it means that for every £100 of such stock £10 additional has to be paid, and the stock is said to be at 10 premium. If, on the other hand, it is quoted at 90, it means that £100 of such stock can be purchased for £90, and the stock is said to stand at a discount of 10. The interest in either case is of course calculated on the face value, that is, £100.

This applies to all kinds of stock on the same principle, the prices varying according to the esteem in which they are held, or, in other words, the credit they have with the moneyed world.

The shares of companies, which are only purchasable in whole numbers, are of various denominations, or face values; and again these face values by no means represent the market value. Shares of £5 each (nominal value) may be quoted as selling at 6, which would be 1 pre- mium, but the dividend or interest would be calculated on £5. On the other hand, a £5 share quoted at 4 would be 1 discount, but the dividend or interest would still be calculated on the face value of £5.

In very many cases the whole of the nominal value of a share is not called up, *i.e.*, is not re- quired to be immediately paid. Thus a £5 share may have only £3 paid upon it, leaving a lia- bility of £2, which the holder may at any time be called upon to pay, whether convenient or not. This should always be borne in mind when purchasing shares of any kind, as the neglect of this precaution has often involved holders in serious difficulties, from being called upon to pay up when least able to do so.

The dividend on shares of this kind is calcu- lated only on the amount paid up.

DIVIDENDS.

A dividend is the sum apportioned periodi- cally, in the shape of profit or interest, to holders of stocks and shares. It may be a fixed sum according to the rate of interest, as in the case of the Funds, Colonial Stocks, &c., or a varying sum according to the profits made, as in the case of railway shares and those of other companies. The dividends on the Funds and some Colonial Stocks are paid quarterly, at the beginning of January, April, July, and October. A month prior to the date of payment the stocks are marked "ex-div.," meaning that any purchase effected after the 1st December, 1st March, 1st June, and 1st September, would not carry that quarter's dividend, as it is held in favour of the person whose name is registered on the books on those dates.

The interest dependent upon the shares or stocks of companies is usually paid half-yearly, after the periodical meeting, when the accounts are presented and the profits declared. A cer- tain date is fixed when these shares and stocks are saleable "ex-div." or "ex-interest."

CHAPTER V. BRITISH GOVERNMENT FUNDS.

THE safest of all investments are those repre- sented by the National Debt of this country, but the rate of interest or annual income derivable therefrom is small. The debt is nominally divided into three parts:- The Funded Debt, the Unfunded Debt, Terminable Annuities.

The Funded Debt (1) is permanent; it is repre- sented by Consols yielding interest at the rate of 2 1/2 per cent. per annum, or £2 10s. a year for every £100 of stock. The Government is not under obligation to redeem the principal at any fixed time, but power is reserved to pay off the loan at *par* (that is at the rate of £100 for every £100 stock, irrespective of its then selling value) in the year 1905. Another debt of compara- tively small amount, bearing interest at 2 3/4 per cent. per annum, may also be paid off at *par* in 1905.

The great bulk of the National Debt, amount- ing to over five hundred millions sterling, is, represented by what, in Stock Exchange *par- lance*, is known as Goschen's Consols, so called from the Chancellor of the Exchequer of that name, to whom is due the conversion of the old "three per cents.," in the year 1888.

This stock bears interest at the rate of 2 3/4 per cent. per annum until the year 1903; from that date it is to be reduced to 2 1/2 per cent. until 1923, when the principal may be paid off at *par*.

There is yet another fixed debt of about forty millions sterling called "Local Loans Stock," being money borrowed by the Government for the purpose of making advances to Corporations for local works. This stock may be redeemed at *par* in 1912.

The Unfunded Debt (2) consists of loans to the Government for temporary purposes. These loans are for various periods varying from seven days to as many years. They are represented by Exchequer Bills, Exchequer Bonds and Trea- sury Bills, which bear interest, according to the value of money at the time they are issued, from day to day. Due notice is given when a loan is to be paid off or renewed, and interest ceases on the day named for redemption.

TERMINABLEANNUITIES.

Terminable Annuities (3) may be regarded as a "Sinking Fund," or means by which a con- siderable portion of the National Debt is paid off every year and "The Funds" proportionately reduced.

Thus the Government is empowered to give an annuity for a certain number of years in ex- change for permanent stock in the Funds. For instance, a holder of £1,000 2 3/4 per cent. stock is receiving £27 10s. a year in the shape of interest. The Government offers to pay double the amount of interest or £55, if the £1,000 stock is trans- ferred to them, and to continue this £55 a year for twenty years and no longer.

At the expiration of that period the interest ceases and the principal sum of £1,000 is struck off the National Debt, which is in consequence reduced by that sum.

LOANS-THEINTERESTONWHICHISGUARAN- TEEDBYTHE BRITISHGOVERNMENT .

These consist of loans to the Government of Canada for railway purposes, upon which 4 per cent. per annum is guaranteed. Also loans to the Colonies of Jamaica at 4 per cent. and Mauri- tius at 3 per cent., to the Egyptian Government at 3 per cent. and to the Turkish Government at 4 per cent.; in this latter case the French Government joins in the guarantee.

These are all perfectly safe investments, so far as the interest or income derived is concerned, but there appears to be no arrangement for the redemption of the loans.

The large loans to the Government of India at 3 1/2 and 3 per cent., repayable in 1931 and 1948, are guaranteed by the Secretary of State for India, practically the British Government.

Any amount may be invested in the above stocks and annuities through the medium of either a banker through his broker, or by a broker direct. The broker's charge for trans- acting in Consols is 25. 6d. (1/8) per cent. on the amount invested, but provincial bankers make a further small charge for guaranteeing the busi- ness, that is, they protect their customer from any loss that may arise owing to the failure of the broker to carry out the contract.

The dividends, interest, or annuity derivable from these investments, may be received by personal application of the holder at the Bank of England on certain fixed days, or on signing a printed form furnished on application by the Bank of England, per post, they will send from time to time without further notice a warrant or order for the amount due, which warrant or order may be paid into a bank account, or, on a proper introduction, cashed at any bank or post office. The simplest plan, however, may be to give your banker a Power of Attorney to receive the divi- dends from time to time and place the amount to the credit of your account.

Income tax is deducted from all dividends; but if a person is not liable to such tax, by reason of the total income coming within the Exemption Clause, the amount can be recovered through a surveyor of taxes, as to which the banker would give all the information required (*).

(*) Such information may also be found in detail in a little handy book, "Income Tax, and how to get it Refunded." 1s. 6d. Pub- lished by Messrs. Effingham, Wilson & Co.

The stock of the Bank of England, which may be purchased in any amount, the same as Consols, is a favourite investment with some, but the price is so high that the income to be derived therefrom is no more, and sometimes even less, than from the Funds.

AUTOMATICRE-INVESTMENTOFDIVIDENDS.

Holders of stock in the Funds who are not desirous of receiving their dividends, but prefer to have them added half-yearly to the capital sum without further action on their part, are granted facilities by which this may be done automatically, on application to the Bank of England. The instructions apply to amounts of stock of less than £1,000 only. These facilities are also extended to holders of Metropolitan Consolidated Stocks, and to the India 3 per cent. and 3 1/2 per cent. stocks.

CHAPTER VI. GOVERNMENT ANNUITIES.

THE Commissioners for the Reduction of the National Debt, under the authority of Parlia- ment, grant annuities either on single lives, or on two lives and the life of the survivor, or on the joint continuance of two lives, such annui- ties to commence immediately. In the case of single lives, the annuity *may* be made to com- mence at a future period, and the consideration for it may be paid by the purchaser annually in sums of money not less than £5, but in case of default in keeping up the annual instalments, all the annual payments previously made are forfeited, and all right to the annuity is ex- tinguished.

Payment for an annuity is made by the transfer of 2 1/2 per cent. Consols, or money of equi- valent value, at the price of the stock on the day of the transaction.

The tables (see p.44) show the annuity which £100 of 2 1/2 per cent. stock will purchase, to con- tinue during the life of a nominee at the re- spective ages and according to the prices of 2 1/2 per cent. stock therein stated. It will be seen that in the case of money being paid for the purchase of the annuity, the higher the price of Consols the dearer will be the purchase. Thus, a female buying an annuity at the age of fifty, amounting to £5 19s. 8d. per annum, and Consols being at *par*, or 100, would, if she paid for it *in money*, have to expend £100. But suppose Consols to be at 108 (as they are at present) she would have to pay £108 for the same annuity.

Tables relating to annuities on joint lives and to deferred annuities may be obtained at the National Debt Office, 19, Old Jewry, London, by application direct, or through a bank.

No person under the age of fifteen can be ap- pointed the nominee for any life annuity.

Life annuities are payable quarterly at the National Debt Office, in the form of a warrant on the Bank of England, either on personal demand, or through a bank by Power of Attor- ney; or they can be transmitted to the pro- prietor by post. The fixed dates are the fifth of January, the fifth of April, the fifth of July, and the fifth of October in each year.

The first quarterly payment of annuities will become due as follows, namely: On annuities purchased between the first of December and the last day of February, on the fifth of April next following the day of purchase.

Between the first of March and the last day of May, on the fifth of July next following.

Between the first of June and the last day of August, on the fifth of October next following.

Between the first of September and the last day of November, on the fifth of January next following.

No sum less than £100 of stock or money can be received in the first instance, but it may be added to subsequently in sums of not less than £20.

Upon the expiration of any life annuity a sum equal to one-fourth of the annuity (over and above all quarterly arrears thereof) will be paid to the representatives of the annuitant, if claimed within two years after such expiration.

Very heavy penalties attach to persons making false statements or declarations in respect of the purchase of an annuity.

Per Acts 10 Geo. IV., cap. 24, and 51 and 52 Vic. cap 15.

TABLE showing the ANNUITY, continuing during the *Life* of any person of the following Ages,

which £100 STOCK in the 2 1/2 PER CENT. BANK ANNUITIES will purchase.

Age of the Nominee	When the price of £100 of 2 1/2 per cent. Stock exclusive of accrued dividend lies between £94 15 9 and £95 13 11.		When the price of £100 of 2 1/2 per cent. Stock exclusive of accrued dividend lies between £95 13 11 and £96 12 5.		When the price of £100 of 2 1/2 per cent. Stock exclusive of accrued dividend lies between £96 12 5 and £97 11 3.		Age of the Nominee
	Male.	Female.	Male.	Female.	Male.	Female.	
	£ s. d.	£ s. d.	£ s. d.	£ s. d.	£ s. d.	£ s. d.	
15	4 1 2	3 15 3	4 1 7	3 15 7	4 2 0	3 15 11	15
16	4 1 10	3 15 9	4 2 3	3 16 1	4 2 8	3 16 6	16
17	4 2 7	3 16 4	4 3 0	3 16 8	4 3 5	3 17 1	17
18	4 3 4	3 16 11	4 3 9	3 17 3	4 4 3	3 17 8	18
19	4 4 2	3 17 6	4 4 7	3 17 11	4 5 0	3 18 3	19
20	4 4 11	3 18 2	4 5 5	3 18 6	4 5 10	3 18 11	20
21	4 5 9	3 18 9	4 6 2	3 19 2	4 6 8	3 19 7	21
22	4 6 7	3 19 5	4 7 1	3 19 10	4 7 6	4 0 3	22
23	4 7 6	4 0 1	4 7 11	4 0 6	4 8 5	4 0 11	23
24	4 8 4	4 0 10	4 8 10	4 1 3	4 9 4	4 1 8	24
25	4 9 3	4 1 6	4 9 9	4 2 0	4 10 3	4 2 5	25
26	4 10 3	4 2 4	4 10 9	4 2 9	4 11 3	4 3 2	26
27	4 11 3	4 3 1	4 11 9	4 3 6	4 12 3	4 4 0	27
28	4 12 3	4 3 11	4 12 9	4 4 4	4 13 3	4 4 10	28
29	4 13 3	4 4 9	4 13 10	4 5 2	4 14 4	4 5 8	29
30	4 14 4	4 5 7	4 14 11	4 6 1	4 15 5	4 6 7	30
31	4 15 6	4 6 6					

|| 4 16 0 | 4 7 0 || 4 16 7 | 4 7 6 || 31 | | 32 || 4 16 7 | 4 7 6 || 4 17 2 | 4 8 0 || 4 17 9 | 4 8 6 || 32 | | 33 || 4 17 10 | 4 8 6 || 4 18 5 | 4 9 0 || 4 19 0 | 4 9 6 || 33 | | 34 || 4 19 0 | 4 9 6 || 4 19 7 | 4 10 0 || 5 0 3 | 4 10 6 || 34 | | 35 || 5 0 4 | 4 10 7 || 5 0 11 | 4 11 1 || 5 1 6 | 4 11 8 || 35 | | 36 || 5 1 8 | 4 11 9 || 5 2 3 | 4 12 3 || 5 2 11 | 4 12 9 || 36 | | 37 || 5 3 0 | 4 12 11 || 5 3 8 | 4 13 5 || 5 4 3 | 4 14 0 || 37 | | 38 || 5 4 5 | 4 14 2 || 5 5 1 | 4 14 8 || 5 5 9 | 4 15 3 || 38 | | 39 || 5 5 11 | 4 15 5 || 5 6 7 | 4 16 0 || 5 7 3 | 4 16 7 || 39 | | 40 || 5 7 6 | 4 16 10 || 5 8 2 | 4 17 5 || 5 8 10 | 4 18 0 || 40 | | 41 || 5 9 1 | 4 18 3 || 5 9 9 | 4 18 10 || 5 10 6 | 4 19 5 || 41 | | 42 || 5 10 9 | 4 19 9 || 5 11 6 | 5 0 4 || 5 12 2 | 5 1 0 || 42 | | 43 || 5 12 6 | 5 1 4 || 5 13 3 | 5 2 0 || 5 14 0 | 5 2 7 || 43 | | 44 || 5 14 5 | 5 3 0 || 5 15 1 | 5 3 8 || 5 15 11 | 5 4 4 || 44 | | 45 || 5 16 4 | 5 4 10 || 5 17 1 | 5 5 6 || 5 17 10 | 5 6 2 || 45 | | 46 || 5 18 4 | 5 6 9 || 5 19 1 | 5 7 5 || 5 19 11 | 5 8 2 || 46 | | 47 || 6 0 6 | 5 8 9 || 6 1 3 | 5 9 6 || 6 2 1 | 5 10 2 || 47 | | 48 || 6 2 9 | 5 10 11 || 6 3 7 | 5 11 8 || 6 4 5 | 5 12 5 || 48 | | 49 || 6 5 2 | 5 13 3 || 6 6 0 | 5 14 0 || 6 6 11 | 5 14 9 || 49 | | 50 || 6 7 8 | 5 15 7 || 6 8 7 | 5 16 5 || 6 9 5 | 5 17 2 || 50 | | 51 || 6 10 5 | 5 18 1 || 6 11 3 | 5 18 11 || 6 12 2 | 5 19 9 || 51 | | 52 || 6 13 3 | 6 0 9 || 6 14 2 | 6 1 7 || 6 15 2 | 6 2 5 || 52 | | 53 || 6 16 4 | 6 3 7 || 6 17 4 | 6 4 5 || 6 18 4 | 6 5 4 || 53 | | 54 || 6 19 8 | 6 6 7 || 7 0 8 | 6 7 6 || 7 1 8 | 6 8 5 || 54 | | 55 || 7 3 2 | 6 9 10 || 7 4 3 | 6 10 8 || 7 5 3 | 6 11 8 || 55 | | 56 || 7 7 0 | 6 13 3 || 7 8 1 | 6 14 2 || 7 9 2 | 6 15 2 || 56 | | 57 || 7 11 2 | 6 17 0 || 7 12 3 | 6 17 11 || 7 13 5 | 6 18 11 || 57 | | 58 || 7 15 8 | 7 0 11 || 7 16 10 | 7 1 11 || 7 18 0 | 7 2 11 || 58 | | 59 || 8 0 7 | 7 5 1 || 8 1 9 | 7 6 2 || 8 3 0 | 7 7 3 || 59 | | 60 || 8 5 10 | 7 9 6 || 8 7 0 | 7 10 8 || 8 8 4 | 7 11 9 || 60 | | 61 || 8 11 3 | 7 14 4 || 8 12 7 | 7 15 6 || 8 13 11 | 7 16 8 || 61 | | 62 || 8 16 11 | 7 19 5 || 8 18 3 | 8 0 7 || 8 19 8 | 8 1 10 || 62 | | 63 || 9 3 0 | 8 4 10 || 9 4 5 | 8 6 1 || 9 5 10 | 8 7 4 || 63 | | 64 || 9 9 5 | 8 10 8 || 9 10 11 | 8 12 0 || 9 12 5 | 8 13 4 || 64 | | 65 || 9 16 3 | 8 17 2 || 9 17 10 | 8 18 6 || 9 19 5 | 8 19 11 || 65 | | 66 || 10 3 6 | 9 4 1 || 10 5 1 | 9 5 6 || 10 6 8 | 9 7 0 || 66 | | 67 || 10 11 0 | 9 11 8 || 10 12 8 | 9 13 2 || 10 14 5 | 9 14 8 || 67 | | 68 || 10 19 0 | 9 19 9 || 11 0 9 | 10 1 4 || 11 2 7 | 10 2 11 || 68 | | 69 || 11 7 8 | 10 8 4 || 11 9 6 | 10 10 0 || 11 11 4 | 10 11 8 || 69 | | 70 || 11 17 0 | 10 17 5 || 11 18 11 | 10 19 1 || 12 0

Age	When the price of £100 of 2½ per cent. Stock exclusive of accrued dividend of the Nominee lies between £97 11 3 and £98 10 6.		When the price of £100 of 2½ per cent. Stock exclusive of accrued dividend of the Nominee lies between £98 10 6 and £99 10 1.		When the price of £100 of 2½ per cent. Stock exclusive of accrued dividend of the Nominee is above £99 10 1.	
	Male.	Female.	Male.	Female.	Male.	Female.
70					11 …	11 0 11
71	12 6 11	11 6 8	12 9 0	11 8 6	12 11 0	11 10 5
72	12 17 8	11 16 5	12 19 10	11 18 4	13 2 0	12 0 4
73	13 9 0	12 6 9	13 11 3	12 8 9	13 13 6	12 10 10
74	14 0 9	12 17 8	14 3 1	12 19 10	14 5 6	13 2 0
75	14 13 0	13 9 4	14 15 6	13 11 7	14 18 0	13 13 10
76	15 6 2	14 1 9	15 8 9	14 4 1	15 11 5	14 6 6
77	15 19 8	14 15 0	16 2 5	14 17 6	16 5 2	15 0 0
78	16 14 0	15 9 0	16 16 10	15 11 8	16 19 9	15 14 4
79	17 9 3	16 4 0	17 12 3	16 6 10	17 15 4	16 9 7
80	18 5 4	16 19 10	18 8 6	17 2 9	18 11 9	17 5 9

Per Acts 10 Geo. IV., cap. 24, and 51 and 52 Vic. cap 15.

TABLE showing the ANNUITY, continuing during the *Life* of any person of the following Ages,

which £100 STOCK in the 2 1/2 PER CENT. BANK ANNUITIES will purchase.

————| | || £ s. d. | £ s. d. || £ s. d. | £ s. d. || £ s. d. | £ s. d. || | | 15 || 4 2 5 | 3 16 4 || 4 2 10 | 3 16 8 || 4 3 3 | 3 17 0 || 15 | | 16 || 4 3 1 | 3 16 10 || 4 3 7 | 3 17 3 || 4 4 0 | 3 17 7 || 16 | | 17 || 4 3 11 | 3 17 5 || 4 4 4 | 3 17 10 || 4 4 9 | 3 18 3 || 17 | | 18 || 4 4 8 | 3 18 0 || 4 5 1 | 3 18 5 || 4 5 7 | 3 18 10 || 18 | | 19 || 4 5 6 | 3 18 8 || 4 5 11 | 3 19 1 || 4 6 5 | 3 19 6 || 19 | | 20 || 4 6 3 | 3 19 4 || 4 6 9 | 3 19 8 || 4 7 3 | 4 0 1 || 20 | | 21 || 4 7 2 | 4 0 0 || 4 7 7 | 4 0 5 || 4 8 1 | 4 0 10 || 21 | | 22 || 4 8 0 | 4 0 8 || 4 8 6 | 4 1 1 || 4 9 0 | 4 1 6 || 22 | | 23 || 4 8 11 | 4 1 4 || 4 9 5 | 4 1 9 || 4 9 11 | 4 2 3 || 23 | | 24 || 4 9 10 | 4 2 1 || 4 10 4 | 4 2 6 || 4 10 10 | 4 3 0 || 24 | | 25 || 4 10 9 | 4 2 10 || 4 11 4 | 4 3 3 || 4 11 10 | 4 3 9 || 25 | | 26 || 4 11 9 | 4 3 7 || 4 12 3 | 4 4 1 || 4 12 10 | 4 4 6 || 26 | | 27 || 4 12 9 | 4 4 3 || 4 13 4 | 4 4 11 || 4 13 10 | 4 5 4 || 27 | | 28 || 4 13 10 | 4 5 3 || 4 14 4 | 4 5 9 || 4 14 11 | 4 6 3 || 28 | | 29 || 4 14 11 | 4 6 2 || 4 15 6 | 4 6 7 || 4 16 0 | 4 7 1 || 29 | | 30 || 4 16 0 | 4 7 0 || 4 16 7 | 4 7 6 || 4 17 2 | 4 8 0 || 30 | | 31 || 4 17 2 | 4 8 0 || 4 17 9 | 4 8 6 || 4 18 4 | 4 9 0 || 31 | | 32 || 4 18 4 | 4 9 0 || 4 18 11 | 4 9 6 || 4 19 6 | 4 10 0 || 32 | | 33 || 4 19 7 | 4 10 0 || 5 0 2 | 4 10 6 || 5 0 10 | 4 11 1 || 33 | | 34 || 5 0 10 | 4 11 1 || 5 1 6 | 4 11 7 || 5 2 1 | 4 12 2 || 34 | | 35 || 5 2 2 | 4 12 2 || 5 2 10 | 4 12 9 || 5 3 5 | 4 13 4 || 35 | | 36 || 5 3 6 | 4 13 4 || 5 4 2 | 4 13 11 || 5 4 10 | 4 14 6 || 36 | | 37 || 5 4 11 | 4 14 7 || 5 5 7 | 4 15 2 || 5 6 4 | 4 15 9 || 37 | | 38 || 5 6 5 | 4 15 10 || 5 7 1 | 4 16 5 || 5 7 10 | 4 17 0 || 38 | | 39 || 5 7 11 | 4 17 2 || 5 8 8 | 4 17 9 || 5_19_ 4 | 4 18 5 || 39 | | 40 || 5 9 6 | 4 18 7 || 5 10 3 | 4 19 2 || 5 11 0 | 4 19 10 || 40 | | 41 || 5 11 3 | 5 0 1 || 5 11 11 | 5 0 8 || 5 12 8 | 5 1 4 || 41 | | 42 || 5 12 11 | 5 1 8 || 5 13 8 | 5 2 3 || 5 14 6 | 5 3 0 || 42 | | 43 || 5 14 9 | 5 3 3 || 5 15 6 | 5 4 0 || 5 16 4 | 5 4 8 || 43 | 44 || 5 16 8 | 5 5 0 || 5 17 6 | 5 5 9 || 5 18 3 | 5 6 5 || 44 | | 45 || 5 18 8 | 5 6 11 || 5_11_ 6 | 5 7 7 || 6 0 4 | 5 8 4 || 45 | | 46 || 6 0 9 | 5 8 10 || 6 1 7 | 5 9 7 || 6 2 5 | 5 10 4 || 46 | | 47 || 6 3 0 | 5 10 11 || 6 3 10 | 5 11 8 || 6 4 8 | 5 12 6 || 47 | | 48 || 6 5 3 | 5 13 2 || 6 6 2 | 5 13 11 || 6 7 1 | 5 14 9 || 48 | | 49 || 6 7 9 | 5 15 6 || 6 8 8 | 5 16 4 || 6 9 7 | 5 17 1 || 49 | | 50 || 6 10 4 | 5 18 0 || 6 11 4 | 5 18 10 || 6 12 3 | 5 19 8 || 50 | | 51 || 6 13 2 | 6 6 6 || 6 14 1 | 6 1 5 || 6 15 1 | 6 2 3 || 51 | | 52 || 6 16 1 | 6 3 3 || 6 17 1 | 6 4 2 || 6 18 1 | 6 5 0 || 52 | | 53 || 6 19 4 | 6 6 2 || 7 0 4 | 6 7 1 || 7 1 5 | 6 8 0

|| 53 | | 54 || 7 2 8 | 6 9 4 || 7 3 9 | 6 10 3 || 7 4 10 | 6 11 2 || 54 | | 55 || 7 6 4 | 6 12 7 || 7 7 5 | 6 13 6 || 7 8 7 | 6 14 6 || 55 | | 56 || 7 10 3 | 6 16 2 || 7 11 5 | 6 17 2 || 7 12 7 | 6 18 2 || 56 | | 57 || 7 14 6 | 7 0 0 || 7 15 9 | 7 1 0 || 7 16 11 | 7 2 1 || 57 | | 58 || 7 19 2 | 7 4 0 || 8 0 5 | 7 5 1 || 8 1 8 | 7 6 2 || 58 | | 59 || 8 4 3 | 7 8 4 || 8 5 6 | 7 9 6 || 8 6 10 | 7 10 7 || 59 | | 60 || 8 9 7 | 7 12 11 || 8 10 11 | 7 14 1 || 8 12 4 | 7 15 3 || 60 | | 61 || 8 15 3 | 7 17 10 || 8 16 7 | 7 19 1 || 8 18 0 | 8 0 4 || 61 | | 62 || 9 1 0 | 8 3 1 || 9 2 6 | 8 4 4 || 9 4 0 | 8 5 8 || 62 | | 63 || 9 7 3 | 8 8 8 || 9 8 9 | 8 10 0 || 9 10 4 | 8 11 4 || 63 | | 64 || 9 13 11 | 8 14 8 || 9 15 6 | 8 16 1 || 9 17 1 | 8 17 6 || 64 | | 65 || 10 1 0 | 9 1 4 || 10 2 7 | 9 2 9 || 10 4 4 | 9 4 3 || 65 | | 66 || 10 8 5 | 9 8 6 || 10 10 1 | 9 10 0 || 10 11 10 | 9 11 6 || 66 | | 67 || 10 16 2 | 9 16 3 || 10 17 11 | 9 17 10 || 10 19 9 | 9 19 6 || 67 | | 68 || 11 4 5 | 10 4 7 || 11 6 3 | 10 6 3 || 11 8 2 | 10 7 11 || 68 | | 69 || 11 13 3 | 10 13 5 || 11 15 3 | 10 15 2 || 11 17 2 | 10 17 0 || 69 | | 70 || 12 2 11 | 11 2 9 || 12 4 11 | 11 4 7 || 12 7 0 | 11 6 6 || 70 | | 71 || 12 13 2 | 11 12 4 || 12 15 4 | 11 14 3 || 12 17 6 | 11 16 3 || 71 | | 72 || 13 4 2 | 12 2 4 || 13 6 5 | 12 4 5 || 13 8 9 | 12 6 6 || 72 | | 73 || 13 15 10 | 12 13 0 || 13 18 2 | 12 15 1 || 14 0 7 | 12 17 4 || 73 | | 74 || 14 7 11 | 13 4 2 || 14 10 5 | 13 6 5 || 14 13 0 | 13 8 9 || 74 | | 75 || 15 0 7 | 13 16 2 || 15 3 2 | 13 18 7 || 15 5 10 | 14 1 0 || 75 | | 76 || 15 14 1 | 14 8 11 || 15 16 10 | 14 11 6 || 15 19 7 | 14 14 0 || 76 | | 77 || 16 8 0 | 15 2 7 || _17_ 10 11 | 15 5 3 || 16 13 10 | 15 7 11 || 77 | | 78 || 17 2 8 | 15 17 0 || 17 5 9 | 15 19 10 || 17 8 10 | 16 2 8 || 78 | | 79 || 17 18 5 | 16 12 6 || 18 1 8 | 16 15 5 || 18 4 10 | 16 18 5 || 79 | | 80 || 18 15 0 | 17 8 10 || 18 18 4 | 17 11 11 || 19 1 9 | 17 15 0 || 80 |

_____

_____

INSURANCE OFFICE ANNUITIES.

Some of the Insurance Offices grant imme- diate annuities. Of course, in purchasing a life annuity from an Insurance Office, it is necessary to ensure as far as is humanly possible that an annuity will be paid for life. This not only de- pends upon the present solvency of the company, but upon that solvency being maintained. There is not much difficulty, however, in selecting from amongst the numerous well-established companies, with proper advice, one that will answer every requirement. The following table shows the amount of an annuity granted by the undermentioned companies for every £100 paid. The age last birthday is that upon which the pay- ment is based, and the initial letters M. and F. indicate the rates for male and female lives. The ages quoted range from 50 to 70 years, but the terms for purchasing an annuity at any age can be obtained at the Insurance Office.

By a few companies, distinguished thus (!), the proportionate amount of annuity is payable to the day of death.

Office		Age 50	Age 52	Age 55	Age 58	Age 60	Age 62	Age 65	Age 70
		£ s. d.	£ s. d.	£ s. d.	£ s. d.	£ s. d.	£ s. d.	£ s. d.	£ s. d.
!British Empire Mutual	M	7 4 6	7 10 2	8 0 2	8 12 10	9 3 2	9 14 6	10 14 4	12 16 4
	F	6 12 0	6 17 0	7 6 2	7 17 4	8 6 2	8 16 2	9 14 4	11 15 10
Caledonian	M	7 6 2	7 12 0	8 2 8	8 16 0	9 7 0	9 19 2	11 0 0	13 5 10
	F	6 11 8	6 17 0	7 6 2	7 17 11	8 7 0	8 15 7	9 13 10	11 14 11
City of Glasgow	M	7 5 6	7 11 6	8 2 0	8 15 6	9 6 6	9 18 6	10 19 0	13 4 6
	F	6 12 6	6 17 6	7 7 5	7 17 9	8 6 7	8 16 0	9 14 10	11 14 7
Eagle	M	7 5 10	7 11 6	8 1 10	8 15 0	9 5 8	9 17 6	10 18 0	13 1 4
	F	6 12 10	6 18 2	7 7 6	7 19 2	8 8 4	8 18 8	9 17 6	12 0 4
Economic	M	7 5 6	7 11 6	8 1 10	8 15 4	9 6 4	9 18 4	10 19 8	13 4 10
	F	6 12 4	6 17 8	7 7 4	7 19 2	8 8 4	8 19 0	9 18 4	12 2 8
Edinburgh	M	7 4 6	7 10 6	8 1 4	8 14 10	9 6 2	9 18 6	11 0 0	12 19

6|M| | |F| 6 11 2| 6 16 8| 7 6 6| 7 18 6| 8 8 0| 8 18 10| 9 18 6|11 17 8|F| | | | | | | | | | | | | |!English and Scottish |M| 7 10 0| 7 16 8| 8 6 10| 8 19 0| 9 10 2|10 2 8|11 3 2|13 6 4|M| | Law |F| 6 12 4| 6 17 4| 7 7 4| 7 19 4| 8 8 6| 8 18 10| 9 18 4|11 19 0|F| | | | | | | | | | | | | |!Friends' Provident |M| 6 15 4| 7 0 10| 7 10 4| 8 1 8| 8 10 7| 9 0 9| 9 18 10|11 18 6|M| | |F| 6 5 8| 6 10 9| 6 19 11| 7 11 1| 7 19 11| 8 9 11| 9 7 1|11 4 7|F| | | | | | | | | | | | | General |M| 7 4 8| 7 11 10| 8 3 10| 8 17 4| 9 7 2| 9 18 8|11 2 0|13 8 6|M| | |F| 6 13 4| 6 18 10| 7 9 2| 8 1 2| 8 10 0| 8 19 6| 9 15 8|11 10 10|F| | | | | | | | | | | | | |!Gresham | | 6 18 5| 7 4 0| 7 14 1| 8 6 7| 8 16 8| 9 7 11|10 8 1|12 12 11| | | | | | | | | | | | | | | |!Guardian |M| 6 19 4| 7 5 4| 7 15 8| 8 9 0| 8 19 8| 9 11 6|10 1 2|12 15 10|M| | |F| 6 6 6| 6 11 10| 7 1 6| 7 13 2| 8 2 4| 8 12 10| 9 11 8|11 14 8|F| | | | | | | | | | | | | |!Hand-in-Hand |M| 7 3 4| 7 9 4| 8 0 0| 8 13 4| 9 4 2| 9 16 2|10 17 0|13 1 4|M| | |F| 6 10 2| 6 15 8| 7 5 4| 7 17 2| 8 6 6| 8 17 0| 9 16 2|11 19 10|F| | | | | | | | | | | | | Law Union and Crown |M| 7 2 8| 7 8 4| 7 18 10| 8 12 0| 9 2 8| 9 14 8|10 15 6|13 0 2|M| | |F| 6 9 10| 6 15 2| 7 4 8| 7 15 10| 8 4 10| 8 15 2| 9 14 2|11 17 6|F| | | | | | | | | | | | | |!Legal and General |M| 7 2 0| 7 7 6| 8 18 6| 8 13 8| 9 5 2| 9 17 6|10 17 10| — |M| | |F| 6 7 10| 6 13 0| 7 2 0| 7 13 0| 8 1 10| 8 12 2| 9 6 8| — |F| | | | | | | | | | | | Life Association of |M| 7 6 0| 7 12 0| 8 2 8| 8 16 0| 9 7 0| 9 19 2|11 0 6|13 4 8|M| | Scotland |F| 6 12 10| 6 18 2| 7 7 10| 7 19 8| 8 9 0| 8 19 10| 9 19 2|12 2 6|F| | | | | | | | | | | | | Liverpool and London |M| 7 4 4| 7 10 6| 8 1 4| 8 15 0| 9 6 4| 9 19 0|11 0 10|13 7 8|M| | and Globe |F| 6 10 10| 6 16 6| 7 6 4| 7 18 4| 8 8 0| 8 19 0| 9 19 0|12 4 10|F| | | | | | | | | | | | | London, Edinburgh, |M| 8 5 0| 8 11 0| 9 1 8| 9 15 4|10 6 8|10 19 2|12 1 2|14 7 10|M| | and Glasgow |F| 7 11 0| 7 16 6| 8 6 2| 8 18 4| 9 8 0| 9 18 10|10 18 8|13 4 10|F| | | | | | | | | | | | | | Marine and General |M| 6 17 3| 7 3 3| 7 13 3| 8 5 0| 8 14 9| 9 7 0|10 10 0|12 12 0|M| | Mutual |F| 6 4 3| 6 9 6| 6 18 9| 7 10 6| 7 19 6| 8 9 6| 9 8 3|11 10 6|F| | | | | | | | | | | | | National Life |M| 7 11 3| 7 17 3| 8 7 11| 9 1 5| 9 12 7|10 4 10|11 6 5|13 12 3|M| | |F| 6 17 9| 7 3 3| 7 13 0| 8 4 11| 8 14 4| 9 5 2|10 4 9|12 9 10|F| | | | | | | | | | | | | National Provident |M| 6 15 4| 7 0 10| 7 10 4| 8 1 8| 8 10 6| 9 0 8| 9 18 10|11 18 6|M| | |F| 6 5 8| 6 10 8| 6 19 10| 7 11 0| 7 19

10| 8 9 10| 9 7 0|11 4 6|F| | | | | | | | | | | | | | North British and |M| 7 5 4| 7 11 4|
8 1 10| 8 15 2| 9 6 2| 9 18 2|10 19 4|13 4 6|M| | Mercantile |F| 6 12 2| 6 17 6|
7 7 2| 7 19 0| 8 8 2| 8 18 10| 9 18 2|12 2 6|F| | | | | | | | | | | | | | |!Northern |M| 7 1
8| 7 7 0| 7 16 6| 8 8 8| 8 18 6| 9 9 4|10 8 6|12 8 8|M| | |F| 6 9 6| 6 14 4| 7 3 0|
7 13 10| 8 2 2| 8 11 10| 9 9 2|11 9 0|F| | | | | | | | | | | | | | |!Pearl |M| 7 9 4| 7 15 8|
8 6 10| 9 0 4| 9 11 0|10 3 2|11 4 6|13 10 6|M| | |F| 7 3 2| 7 9 4| 8 0 2| 8 13 0| 9
3 0| 9 14 6|10 14 6|12 17 6|F| | | | | | | | | | | | | | Positive |M| 7 0 0| 7 8 0| 8 0 0| 8
15 0| 9 5 0| 9 19 0|11 0 0|13 5 0|M| | |F| 6 10 0| 6 16 0| 7 5 0| 8 0 0| 8 10 0| 9
0 0| 9 15 0|11 15 0|F| | | | | | | | | | | | | | |!Provident Clerks' |M| 6 15 10| 7 1 6| 7
11 9| 8 4 9| 8 15 1| 9 6 9|10 6 10|12 9 5|M| | |F| 6 3 3| 6 8 7| 6 17 10| 7 9 1| 7
18 1| 8 8 5| 9 7 0|11 8 7|F| | | | | | | | | | | | | | Prudential |M| 6 16 6| 7 2 6| 7 13 6|
8 7 0| 8 18 0| 9 10 6|11 12 0|12 17 0|M| | |F| 6 3 0| 6 9 0| 6 19 0| 7 11 0| 8 0 6|
8 11 0| 9 11 0|11 15 0|F| | | | | | | | | | | | | |!Rock |M| 7 5 0| 7 11 2| 8 2 2| 8 16 2|
9 7 9|10 0 5|11 2 11|13 4 2|M| | |F| 6 11 4| 6 17 0| 7 6 11| 7 19 4| 8 9 0| 9 0
2|10 0 6|12 1 3|F| | | | | | | | | | | | | | Royal |M| 6 12 7| 6 18 11| 7 9 5| 8 1 8| 8 11
2| 9 2 2|10 1 10|12 1 0|M| | |F| 6 5 3| 6 11 0| 7 0 7| 7 11 3| 7 19 6| 8 8 8| 9 5
0|10 17 9|F| | | | | | | | | | | | | | Royal Exchange |M| 6 16 11| 7 2 9| 7 13 0| 8 5
11| 8 16 6| 9 8 1|10 8 5|12 11 3|M| | |F| 6 4 3| 6 9 6| 6 18 11| 7 10 5| 7 19 5| 8
9 8| 9 8 3|11 10 7|F| | | | | | | | | | | | | | Scottish Amicable |M| 7 0 7| 7 6 2| 7 16
5| 8 9 2| 8 19 4| 9 11 1|10 11 10|12 15 7|M| | |F| 6 7 8| 6 13 2| 7 2 8| 7 13 9| 8
2 5| 8 12 9| 9 12 0|11 14 1|F| | | | | | | | | | | | | | Scottish Life |M| 7 7 6| 7 13 6| 8
4 4| 8 17 10| 9 9 0|10 1 2|11 2 8|13 8 6|M| | |F| 6 13 6| 6 19 0| 7 8 8| 8 0 8| 8
10 0| 9 0 8|10 0 0|12 2 6|F| | | | | | | | | | | | | | Scottish Metropolitan |M| 7 10 10|
7 18 0| 8 9 4| 9 2 0| 9 11 8|10 3 6|11 5 8|13 11 11|M| | |F| 6 12 9| 6 17 9| 7 6
8| 7 17 6| 8 6 1| 8 16 3| 9 14 6|11 15 8|F| | | | | | | | | | | | | | Scottish Provident
|M| 7 2 8| 7 8 5| 7 18 9| 8 11 11| 9 2 8| 9 14 6|10 15 3|12 16 10|M| | |F| 6 9 8|
6 15 0| 7 4 4| 7 15 11| 8 5 1| 8 15 6| 9 14 5|11 14 3|F| | | | | | | | | | | | | |!Scottish
Widows' Fnd. |M| 6 8 0| 6 13 4| 7 2 2| 7 12 10| 8 1 0| 8 10 6| 9 7 10|11 8 6|M|
| |F| 6 2 6| 6 7 6| 6 16 0| 7 6 2| 7 14 0| 8 3 2| 8 19 10|10 18 6|F| | | | | | | | | | | | | |
Standard |M| 6 19 4| 7 5 0| 7 15 1| 8 7 10| 8 18 5| 9 10 0|10 10 3|12 7 9|M| |

|F| 6 9 8| 6 15 0| 7 4 4| 7 16 0| 8 5 1| 8 15 6| 9 14 5|11 7 1|F| | | | | | | | | | | | | |

Star |M| 7 3 9| 7 10 6| 8 2 1| 8 15 8| 9 5 5| 9 16 7|10 17 2|13 0 1|M| | |F| 6 14 4| 6 19 11| 7 9 6| 8 0 11| 8 9 11| 9 0 1| 9 18 6|11 15 8|F| | | | | | | | | | | | | | Sun (of India) |M| 7 5 10| 7 12 0| 8 2 10| 8 16 8| 9 8 0|10 0 4|11 2 2|13 8 8|M| | |F| 6 12 6| 6 18 0| 7 7 10| 8 0 0| 8 9 8| 9 0 8|10 0 6|12 6 0|F| | | | | | | | | | | | | United Kingdom |M| 6 15 0| 7 0 6| 7 10 3| 8 2 6| 8 15 11| 9 3 3|10 0 3|12 1 0|M| | Temperance |F| 6 2 11| 6 8 0| 6 16 11| 7 6 5| 7 16 4| 8 6 0| 9 3 4|11 2 3|F| | | | | | | | | | | | | Yorkshire |M| 7 1 2| 7 7 6| 7 18 0| 8 10 4| 9 0 0| 9 11 6|10 11 0|12 15 0|M| | |F| 6 8 0| 6 13 6| 7 2 0| 7 12 6| 8 2 6| 8 13 6| 9 12 0|11 12 0|F| | | | | | | | | | | | | |——————————————|-|————|————|————|

———————|————|————|————|————|————|—————|-| | Post Office (Govt.) |M| 6 13 4| 6 19 2| 7 9 10| 8 3 2| 8 14 0| 9 6 0|10 6 10|12 10 10|M| | Anns. |F| 6 0 6| 6 6 0| 6 15 8| 7 7 6| 7 16 8| 8 7 4| 9 6 4|11 9 6|F| | | | | | | | | | | |——————————————|-|————|————|————|

————————|————|————|————|—————|-| | Equitable, U. States} |M| 7 10 0| 7 15 9| 8 6 2| 8 19 3| 9 9 10|10 1 9|11 1 8|12 17 11|M| | Mutual, New York } |F| 6 16 9| 7 2 1| 7 11 6| 8 3 1| 8 12 1| 9 2 8|10 0 9|11 17 8|F| | New York } | | | | | | | | | | | |

INDIAN GOVERNMENT STOCKS.

These stocks stand as high in the estimation of the public as the British Government Funds. They consist of loans raised in this country for the use of the Indian Government and are two in number, bearing interest respectively at the rate of 3 and 3 1/2 per cent.

There is also what is termed a Rupee Paper Loan, raised in India at 3 1/2 per cent. per annum. The interest is paid in the currency of the coun- try, which is the rupee, and that coin being worth only a little more than half its nominal value in this country, the investor in this stock would receive in the shape of interest little more than half the £3 10s. a year. The price of the stock in the market is consequently in the same proportion, and at the present moment is about £62 for every £100 stock.

CHAPTER VII. LOANS TO CORPORATIONS AND COUNTIES OF THE UNITED KINGDOM.

THESE are loans raised by boroughs and coun- ties, and other authorities in this country, for local purposes, upon the security of the rates or other assured income. Before the money is borrowed the consent of the Local Government Board is necessary to make the loan legal, and evidence is required that the resources of the borrowers are ample to meet their obligations.

On most of these stocks the rate of interest is 3 per cent., though there are some few at 3 1/2 per cent. The principal is redeemable at fixed dates, or by a sinking fund, that is, by setting aside so much a year to pay off the loan at a fixed time, or as opportunity offers. For instance, in times when money is scarce or dear there is a proba- bility of these stocks falling below their par value, and the Sinking Fund is then used to buy the stock in the market. Thus the Corporation may be able in effect to pay off a loan of £100 for £90 or £95, whatever the price may be, and so gain the amount of the difference.

Investments in securities of this kind may be considered absolutely safe, although certainly there is the contingent risk of a town, after bor- rowing up to its full powers, drifting into decay from the loss of its staple trade, and so finding itself unable to meet its obligations. The in- vestor should, however, find no difficulty in discovering where such a contingency would be possible.

The interest on these loans is usually sent direct to the stock-holders, by means of an order on a bank.

COLONIAL GOVERNMENT SECURITIES.

Loans made to the various Colonies of Great Britain have always been a favourite mode of investing money, as they command a better rate of interest, at least they have done so in the past, although the confidence which the Colonies have succeeded in inspiring now enables them to borrow money at a low rate of interest. At the same time the old stocks have advanced to a very considerable premium.

Experience has shown that, so far, the invest- ment has been a safe one, although great fluc- tuations have from time to time taken place in the value of some of the stocks, owing to a check in prosperity, depression of trade, or diminished confidence in the stability of the Colony from various causes. These transient clouds have, however, in time, passed away, and confidence has again been established.

The investor should be able readily to distin- guish between those Colonies which are perma- nently settled and not likely to be seriously affected by any passing crisis, and others in a less fortunate or advanced position. And he would do well, if adversity should at any time overtake a Colony, and so send down the value of its stock, to avoid selling out in a panic, but to consider whether the circumstances are such that the crisis may pass off at no distant date, and confidence be restored. It should be remem- bered that there are always speculators who, at such times, endeavour to intensify a crisis, in order that prices may be forced down, and that they may be thereby enabled to acquire stocks at low prices from timid holders.

There are two modes of investing in these securities,

1. Inscribed or Registered Stock.
2. Bonds.

In the case of Inscribed or Registered Stock, any amount can be invested, and the same is registered in the books of the Bank of England or elsewhere, in the name of the investor, in the same way as the Government Funds. The divi- dend or interest is sent to the owner's address by an order payable at a bank, half-yearly or quarterly, as the case may be, or it may, on written instructions being sent to the agents, be transmitted to the credit of the account of the holder at his own bankers periodically. This is by far the best plan; it saves trouble and risk, and, for the matter of that, something in postage. It is, moreover, the method much preferred by the agents themselves, and it involves no additional expense.

The following is a list of the Inscribed Stocks of the Colonial Governments, with an example of the way in which the market price, which of course varies almost from day to day, is quoted:-

COLONIAL   GOVERNMENT   INSCRIBED   STOCKS.

————————- | | | | | | | | | | 1 | 2 | 3 | 4 | 5 | 6 | 7 | 8 | | | | | | | | | | |————————|
—————————|————————————-|—————-|——-|

————————— | £ | £ | | | | | | | | 100,000| 100,000| 1 Mar. 1 Sept.| 4 Aug. | 4
|Antigua 4% Inscribed Stock | 1919-44 | 115 - 117 | | 375,000| 375,000|15

	Stock	Due	Price		Amount Created	Amount Issued	Interest Due	Transfer Books Close
							Mar. 15 Sept.	17 Aug.
3 1/2	Barbados 3 1/2% Inscribed Stock	1925-42	109 - 111		1,120,000	969,940	1 Jan. 1 July	16 Dec.
3	British Columbia (Province of) 3% Insc. Stock	1941	101 - 103		—	194,500	15 Jan. 15 July	16 Dec.
4	British Guiana 4% Inscribed	1935	118 - 120		7,505,800	7,505,800	1 May 1 Nov.	19 Oct.
4	Canada 4% Stock Registered	1904-4-6-8	105 - 111		3,975,614	3,975,614	1 Jan. 1 July	15 Dec.
4	Do. 4% Reduced (late 5%) Registered	1910	109 - 111		4,550,300	4,550,300	1 June Dec.	16 Nov.
3 1/2	Do. 3 1/2% Stock Registered	1909-34	107 - 109		3,431,700	3,431,700	1 Jan. July	15 Dec.
4	Do. 4% Loan for £4,000,000	1910-35	110 - 112		10,939,834	9,978,021	" "	"
3	Do. 3% Stock Registered	1938	102 - 104		3,000,000	2,115,152	1 June 1 Dec.	16 Nov.
4	Cape of Good Hope 4% Stock Registered	1917-23	117 - 119		3,769,465	3,769,465	" "	"
4	Do. (Loan of 1883) Inscribed	1923	119 - 121		9,997,566	9,997,566	15 Apl. 15 Oct.	2 Oct.
4	Do. 4% Consolidated Stk. Ins.	1916-36	116 - 118		—	5,154,272	1 Jan. 1 July	16 Dec.
3 1/2	Do. 3 1/2% Consolidated Ins. Stk.	1929-49	115 - 117		1,076,100	1,070,100	15 Feb. 15 Aug.	16 Jan.
4	Ceylon 4% Inscribed Stock	1934	123 - 125		1,450,000	1,450,000	1 May 1 Nov.	2 Oct.
3	Do. 3% Inscribed Stock	1940	104 - 106		123,670	123,670	15 May 15 Nov.	16 Oct.
4	Grenada 4% Inscribed Stock	1917-42	115 - 117		341,800	341,800	15 April 15 Oct.	16 Sept.
3 1/2	Hong Kong 3 1/2% Inscribed Stock	1918-43	107 - 110		—	1,086,241	16 Feb. 16 Aug.	16 Jan.
4	Jamaica 4% Inscribed Stock	1934	120 - 122		480,749	480,759	1 Feb. 1 Aug.	2 Jan.
4	Mauritius 4% Inscribed Stock	1937	121 - 123		—	282,481	15 May 15 Nov.	16 Oct.
4	Natal 4% Consolidated Stock, Inscribed	1927	120 - 122		3,026,444	3,026,444	1 April 1 Oct.	1 Sept.
4	Do. do. do.	1937	123 - 125		3,714,917	3,714,917	1 June 1 Oct.	3 Nov.
3 1/2	Do. 3 1/2% Inscribed Stock	1914-39	107.5-108.5		320,000	320,000	1 Jan. 1 July	16 Dec.
4	Newfoundland Inscribed	1913-38	109 - 111			550,000		

550,000| " " | " | 4 | Do. 4% Inscribed Stock | 1935 | 110 - 112 | | 200,000| 200,000| " " | " | 4 | Do. 4% Consolidated Stock Inscribed | 1936 | 110 - 112 |

| 9,686,300| 9,686,300| 1 Jan. 1 July | 2 Dec. | 4 |New South Wales Stock, Inscribed | 1933 | 120 - 122 | |16,500,000|16,500,000| 1 April 1 Oct. | 2 Sept.|3 1/2| Do. 3 1/2% Stock, Inscribed | 1924 | 110 - 111 | | — |12,826,200| 1 Mar. 1 Sept.| 5 Aug. |3 1/2| Do. 3 1/2% Stock, Inscribed | 1918 | 109 - 110 | | 4,000,000| 4,000,000| 1 April 1 Oct. | 2 Sept.| 3 | Do. 3% Inscribed Stock | 1935 |101.5-102.5| |29,150,302|29,150,302| 1 May 1 Nov. | 2 Oct. | 4 |New Zealand 4% Consolidated Stock Inscribed | 1929 | 115 - 116 | | 5,960,588| 5,960,588| 1 Jan. 1 July | 2 Dec. |3 1/2| Do. 3 1/2% Stock | 1940 |105.5-106.5| | 1,527,000| 1,526,620| 1 April 1 Oct. | 2 Sept.| 3 | Do. 3% Inscribed | 1945 |100.5-101.5| |10,866,900|10,866,900| 1 Jan. 1 July | 2 Dec. | 4 |Queensland Stock Inscribed | 1915-24 | 113 - 115 | | 8,516,734| 8,516,734| " " | " |3 1/2| Do. 3 1/2% Inscribed | 1921-4-30 |105.5-106.5| | 1,250,000| 1,250,000| " " | " |3 1/2| Do. 3 1/2% do. | 1945 |107.5-108.5| | 85,490| 85,480|15 Feb. 15 Aug. | 16 Jan. | 4 |St. Lucia 4% Inscribed Stock | 1919-44 | 112 - 114 | | 7,721,000| 7,721,000| 1 April 1 Oct. | 11 Sept.| 4 |S. Australia (Loans of 1882-3-4-5-6-7) Reg. | 1916-36 | 112 - 114 | | 2,850,713| 2,517,800| 1 Jan. 1 July | 14 Dec. |3 1/2| Do. 3 1/2% Inscribed Stock Registered | 1939 | 111 - 113 | | 839,500| 839,500| " " | " | 3 | Do. 3% do. do. | 1916-26 | 97.5- 98.5| | 3,546,500| 3,546,500| 1 Jan. 1 July | 16 Dec. |3 1/2|Tasmanian 3 1/2% Inscribed Stock | 1920-40 | 106 - 108 | | 1,000,000| 1,000,000| " " | " | 4 | Do. 4% do. | 1920-40 | 114 - 116 | | 100,000| 100,000|15 Mar. 15 Sept.| 17 Aug. | 4 |Trinidad 4% Inscribed Stock | 1917-42 | 114 - 116 | | 3,365,300| 3,365,300| 1 Jan. 1 July | 16 Dec. | 4 |Victoria 4% Railway Loan, 1881, Inscrib. Stock | 1907 | 106 - 108 | | 9,358,200| 9,358,200| 1 April 1 Oct. | 16 Sept.| 4 | Do. Loans of 1882-3-4, Inscrib. Stock |1908-13-19 | 107 - 113 | | 6,000,000| 6,000,000| 1 Jan. 1 July | 16 Dec. | 4 | Do. Loan of 1885, Inscribed Stock | 1920 | 112 - 114 |

|12,000,000|12,000,000| " " | " |3 1/2| Do. 3 1/2% Inscribed Stock | 1921-3-6 |104.5-105.5| | 2,107,000| 2,107,000| " " | " | 4 | Do. 4% Inscribed Stock | 1911-26 | 108 - 110 | | 961,277| 961,277|15 Jan. 15 July | 16 Dec. | 4 |Western Australia 4% Inscribed Stock | 1934 | 121 - 123 | | 1,876,000| 1,876,000|15 April 15 Oct. | 2 Oct. | 4 | Do. 4% Inscribed Stock | 1911-31 | 112 - 114 | | 750,000| 750,000| 1 May 1 Nov. | 16 Oct. |3 1/2| Do. 3 1/2% Inscribed Stock | 1915-35 | 110 - 112 | | 750,000| 750,000| " " | " | 3 | Do. 3% Inscribed Stock | 1915-35 | 98 - 99 | | | | | | | | | | |

_____

_____

—————- The numbered columns are explained as follows:- 1. The amount of Loan authorized to be raised. | 5. The rate of interest on the Loan. 2. The amount actually owing. | 6. The name of the country borrowing. 3. When the interest is payable. | 7. When the Loan is re-payable - thus "1919 or 1944." 4. When ex interest. | 8. The price for every £100 of stock.

Colonial Government Bonds, the other form of investment, are paper or parchment docu- ments, on which are printed all details of the par- ticular loan taken up by the Colony, the nature of the Security the lender has in advancing his money, the rate of interest, and when and how the principal is to be repaid. These bonds are payable to bearer, and pass from hand to hand without any formal transfer, so that as much care is necessary in safe-keeping them, as with bank-notes. Attached to these bonds are little coupons or slips of paper, each one representing a half or quarter year's interest, from the date of purchase to the time when the principal is to be paid off. The coupon bears the name of the bank or agency where it may be cashed, and any banker will negotiate it. Of course, only the coupon for the interest actually due on the date indicated on the face must be cut off.

FOREIGN GOVERNMENT STOCKS.

These represent money borrowed by various foreign countries on the security of their credit or solvency, and the loans stand to them in the same relationship as the British Government Funds do to this country. The debts are chiefly repre- sented by bonds, the same as Colonial Govern- ment Bonds, and with coupons attached, which, whether payable in England or their own country, are collected by bankers in the same manner. Such European States as Germany, France, Russia, Denmark, Sweden, and Italy, always enjoy good credit, and they may be con- sidered responsible for their financial engage- ments. In the case of Italy, however, it must be remembered that the Italian income-tax, amounting to 20 per cent., is deducted from the interest, which has also to bear the English income-tax, whatever at the time it may be.

When investing in Colonial or Foreign bonds, especial care is necessary in observing the con- ditions of re-payment. Sometimes it is at the option of the borrower, but usually at a certain specified date. Neglect of this precaution may lead to an investor purchasing at a premium, and sooner than expected being paid off at par.

Some of these loans, too, are paid off by annual instalments, lots being drawn to deter- mine the bonds to be redeemed. If the bonds, therefore, have been bought at a premium, there is always the risk of their being drawn for pay- ment and paid off at par. On the other hand, if the bonds are bought at a discount, there is no danger of loss; and a profit will be realised should they be drawn for payment.

For instance, a £100 bond is purchased at 4 premium, costing £104. If the bond is paid off at par, or £100, there is obviously a loss of £4; but if the bond is purchased at 4 discount, cost- ing £96, it is equally obvious that, if paid off at par, there would be a gain of £4.

RAILWAYS.

Next to the British Government Funds, by far the largest amount of money is invested in Eng- lish railways. First in order of safety, as an investment, is the debenture stock of a railway company. This is the first charge on the rail- way, and holders of the stock are paid the in- terest thereon in priority to all other stocks. In the event of the failure of the company they must also be fully satisfied as to principal and interest before any one else can receive a penny. Any amount of stock, odd or even, may be pur- chased through a banker or broker, and war- rants for the interest are forwarded half-yearly to the address of the registered holder. The debenture stocks of good English railways com- mand a high premium, and the investment, therefore, though undoubtedly safe, does not yield much in the way of interest. Guaran- teed stocks are of various kinds and rank — some on the same level as, and others next in order to, debenture stocks. In some cases the interest is guaranteed by another railway. Before investing in these stocks the nature of the guarantee should be ascertained and its value taken into consideration. Preference stocks and shares come next in rank as an invest- ment. The interest on these is fixed at a cer- tain rate per cent., and, after satisfying the preceding stocks, must be paid in full; or if there is not sufficient profit in the year to pay in full, then as much as means will allow. But any deficiency cannot be carried on to the next year, and so it is lost to the holders.

There are several degrees of Preference stock, some taking precedence of others as to interest; a first preference may be as good as debenture stock, whilst the last preference of the same railway company may be no better than ordinary stock.

Preference stock may be purchased in any amount in the market, and the interest war- rants are sent half-yearly to the registered holders.

Ordinary stocks depend on the profits for the year for the interest they yield, and thus afford a wide field for speculation. The stocks of the great English lines may be relied upon as a good investment, the profits being steady and sufficient to assure a fair amount of interest after satisfying the prior claims of debenture and preference stocks.

Ordinary stock may also be purchased in any amount, and the warrants for interest are sent half-yearly to registered holders of stock.

In all cases railway warrants of every kind will, upon written request to the secretary of the railway company, be forwarded periodically to the bankers of the holder of the stock for the credit of his or her account.

INDIAN RAILWAY STOCKS.

These are a favourite investment with the British public. They consist of Debenture, Guaranteed, and Ordinary stocks. The Deben- ture stocks are similar to those of British rail- ways, and are a first charge on the undertaking. The Guaranteed stocks are those upon which there is an undertaking by the Secretary of State for India that the interest shall not be less at any time than they are stated to bear; any deficiency in the earnings being made up by the Government. Should the earnings be more than sufficient to pay the stated interest, the surplus is divided between the Government and the railway company. Annuities may be purchased in some of these railways, that is to say, by paying, we will assume, £30 as the market price, an annuity of £1 a year will be granted for a certain number of years. In dealing with these it is necessary to ascertain when the annuity ceases, or the investor, hav- ing sunk the capital sum, may cease to receive any income therefrom when least expected.

Warrants for interest on these stocks are periodically sent to registered holders.

AMERICAN RAILWAYS.

The stocks and shares of Canadian and American railways offer a more remunerative return than English railways, as they may be purchased at much lower prices. They are subject, however, to speculative influences of many sorts, and can hardly be recommended for safe permanent investment.

No venture should certainly be made in these stocks without full knowledge of the position and prospects of the railway company and the contingencies to which it may be subject. Any banker would obtain for a customer all the in- formation that could be afforded in regard to these stocks, and indicate their market value as an investment, apart from the fictitious value induced by speculators, and the manoeuvres of syndicates and wire-pullers.

FOREIGN RAILWAYS.

The capital of foreign railways consists of obligations, stocks, and shares. The obligations are in the form of bonds, being a first charge on the railway. The bonds vary in amount, but chiefly represent £100 and £20, and they bear a certain rate of interest. Some of the Conti- nental railways may offer a fair investment in this way, but great care is required in the selection.

The stocks and shares of some of the South American railways command a high premium, but of the whole number quoted in the official list the large majority show a heavy decline on the original value, many indeed being valueless. These stocks are highly speculative and subject to be affected by political convulsions and other contingencies, which make them undesirable as an investment.

BANKS.

A joint-stock bank is composed of a number of proprietors who hold the shares which make up the capital of the bank, and to the nominal amount of these shares their liability is limited.

The whole of this amount, however, is not paid up, but only sufficient for the working re- quirements of the bank, the remainder being held in reserve for contingencies. Let us take, for instance, the London and Westminster Bank, which has the largest capital of all the joint- stock banks.

The capital amounts to £14,000,000, made up of 140,000 shares of £100 each. Only £20 of this £100 is paid up, leaving a liability of £80 on every share.

A joint-stock bank is governed by a board of directors, elected by the shareholders; and managers and other officers are appointed by the board to conduct the business. Many of these banks, besides having a head establish-ment in London, have branches all over the country. Every joint-stock bank is compelled by law to publish its accounts so as to show its position, and these accounts are presented to a yearly or half-yearly meeting of the shareholders for approval.

The British Colonies have a good many joint- stock banks, with agencies in London. By a Permissive Act passed in 1825 the shareholders in most of these are liable for double the amount of their shares.

The profits of banking have been, in times past, very large, and the original shareholders of the older banks have reaped the advantage thereof, but bank shares of good repute are not now to be obtained except at a high premium.

The dividends are sent half-yearly to the ad- dress of the shareholders, and they are not liable to income-tax, as the bank pays this. Any one entitled to exemption from income-tax can claim from the surveyor of taxes the amount the bank has paid in respect of the dividend, on a certifi- cate from the bank to that effect.*

* See Note, p.39.

Individuals of a timorous disposition, if they value their peace of mind, would do well to avoid investing their money in bank shares. There are banks whose position and stability are above suspicion, and which return handsome dividends to their shareholders; but there have been cases of banks, enjoying unlimited confi- dence, which have unexpectedly collapsed and overwhelmed their shareholders in ruin. The nervous person, therefore, who could not read of the collapse of a bank without a fearful appre- hension that his own would be the next to go, had better be content with a smaller rate of in- terest and a tranquil mind therewith. The more sanguine investor who desires a good rate of interest for his money, and has a contempt for contingencies, should at least have some know- ledge of accounts, and be able to form some estimate of the position of a bank from the annual balance-sheet, and should carefully ascertain what immediate contingent *liability he would be* subject to in the event of collapse.

COLONIAL AND FOREIGN CORPORATION STOCKS.

These represent money borrowed by munici- palities and trusts in Colonial and foreign towns, and the security offered consists of rates and revenues from the various undertakings, such as harbours, gas, and water-works, city improve- ments, &c., in which the loans are invested. The loans are mostly represented by bonds, to which coupons are attached for interest, and are repayable at a certain specified date. Although they do not command the high credit of British Corporation loans, yet some of the Colonial towns are in fair repute as an investment, and the rate of interest is high enough to tempt a large amount of money from this country. Towns of some size in our Colonies, and thoroughly settled, may be relied upon to carry out their obligations, but mushroom cities and foreign places liable to political fluctuations should be looked upon with suspicion.

CANALS AND DOCKS.

These offer but a limited area for investment. They were formerly very popular with the British investor, but rival interests and labour troubles have affected the confidence in which they were held, and the ordinary stocks are mostly at a considerable discount.

Gas and electric lighting companies, trams and omnibus companies, telegraphs, telephones, water-works, &c., must all be judged by the localities which they serve and the amount of business they are likely to command. As per- manent investments it should be considered whether they are likely to suffer by supersession or opposition, and if they are managed by a trustworthy competent board of directors.

BREWERIES.

Among the numerous commercial undertak- ings offering for investment, brewery companies form a class of themselves, and, with few excep- tions, the English companies appear to have done well, and the shares of the best of them stand at a high premium. Properly managed and dealing in an article of universal consump- tion, brewery companies ought to be a trust-worthy investment: but they are liable to much fluctuation. The shares of one of the leading concerns, which now stand at about 150 for the £100 share, were only four years ago as low as 28, and at the same time only half the interest was paid on the preference shares. American brewery companies are liable to be manipulated by cliques and syndicates, and should be avoided as an investment.

COMMERCIAL AND INDUSTRIAL COMPANIES.

Speaking generally, taking shares in this class of property is like purchasing tickets in a lottery in which the prizes are not numerous. It may fairly be said that at least three-quarters of these companies are formed for the purpose of relieving private owners of concerns which were on the verge of failure through some cause or another.

It would be palpably foolish for a man or a firm doing a prosperous business to give it up into other hands, unless such a price could be obtained for it as would be almost ruinous to the purchaser. True it is that in the remaining quarter may be found perfectly legitimate un- dertakings formed into companies, owing to the death of the owner, deficient capital, or some other valid reason. Some of these flourish and take root, others are prosperous for a time and gradually die out. After a time it will be found that few remain which could be recommended for a permanent investment; and much informa- tion has to be sought and acquired before the venture should be made.

There are, of course, many persons who have the means of acquiring reliable information about a company, and are able to form a sound opinion as to its prospects, but the information is derived from personal knowledge and not from kind friends or from public prints, which are not always to be trusted. These persons purchase shares either for investment or as a speculation — in this latter case with a know-ledge or, at all events, a safe presumption that they will go to a premium, that is, rise in value to considerably more than their nominal amount, either from their own merits, or from an active demand for them on the part of the public, or by artificial stimulation. The holders know pretty well when the highest price has been reached, and then sell out with great advantage to them-selves. It is often at that moment that the *tyro* is recommended to buy, or is seized with a desire to have a share in so good a concern, and parts with his money. The knowing speculator has taken his profit, and sees with grim satisfaction the shares gradually declining in value, until they arrive at the position of more than one-third of existing companies which are now quoted at a discount.

FINANCIAL LAND AND INVESTMENT COMPANIES.

These companies are mostly formed for the purpose of employing their capital in the Colonies, where money commands a higher rate of interest, and can be more profitably employed than in this country.

Some of the older concerns have been suc-cessful, but of the whole number of existing companies at least one-half, judging from the price of their shares, have been failures. The difficulty with these concerns would seem to be the want of direct control, their business having chiefly to be conducted by agents who often consider their own interests before their employers'. Some of these companies appear to have advanced large sums of money on the security of land which they can neither sell nor let, and which has been abandoned by the borrower.

FINANCIAL TRUSTS.

The shares in these trusts were at one time much sought after as an investment. The ostensible business of a trust company is to purchase shares and stocks of other concerns at favourable opportunities, and to invest widely in foreign and other companies offering good dividends, so as to average a high rate of inter- est. They are divided into debenture stock, preferred stock, and deferred stock. The latter has its share of the profits after the others have been satisfied, and at present three-fourths of the companies now doing business have their deferred shares at a discount. The financial collapse in Argentine, some years since, very seriously affected most of these concerns, and it is doubtful, in view of the risky nature of the business, whether they will ever come into favour again.

INSURANCE COMPANIES.

Under the head of Life, Fire, and Marine Insurance, these companies, as a class, have been more steadily successful than others. Most of these concerns are making large profits, and their shares command a high premium; so high, indeed, that an investment at current prices yields but a moderate rate of interest. The risks undertaken by insurance offices are enor- mous in extent, but the law of average by which they are conducted is so accurate that, taken in the long run, and with sufficient business main- tained, misfortune is almost impossible. In all cases, however, so little is called up of the nominal amount of their shares, that a very large liability attaches to them.

STEAMSHIP COMPANIES.

Judging from the prices of the shares in these companies, they have not been very successful as a whole, and it would appear that a Govern- ment subsidy for mail or other service is almost necessary to make them profitable.

MINES.

Speculation in shares of mining companies has of late years been indulged in to an enor- mous extent, and large fortunes have been made and much money lost. As a rule the prizes have been secured by those behind the scenes, and the public have not had the opportunity of participating until the price of shares had reached a figure which was almost prohibitory. As an investment mining shares, even of the best, are not to be recommended. Mines are apt to get worked out when the source of income fails and there is an end to the concern. More- over, hundreds of companies are promoted which have a specious appearance on the prospectus, and are puffed in every imaginable way, when they have not an ounce of ore or a yard of ground to call their own. Of course, there are genuine undertakings which answer well and yield large profits, but it is extremely difficult to discriminate between the good and the bad, and the best after all are but a speculation.

CHAPTER VIII. THE STOCK EXCHANGE.

THE Stock Exchange is a market for the sale and purchase of all kinds of securities. The buildings, wherein business is transacted, occupy a triangular plot of ground near the Bank of England, and comprise the Hall where the various markets are held, and other rooms and offices for the use of the numerous officials. There are 2,500 members, and the management is vested in a Committee selected from their number. Admission to membership is open to any person not engaged in another business, and who is properly proposed and seconded; but very strict regulations and guarantees are enforced before entry, so as to exclude any one whose circumstances and character will not bear the strictest investigation. The hours of busi- ness are eleven to four o'clock on all days except Saturday, when they are until two o'clock. The members of the house are divided into Jobbers and Brokers, the former being dealers in stocks and shares. It is contrary to practice for brokers to deal with brokers, and all trans- actions are between brokers and jobbers.

What are known as "markets" are groups of jobbers distributed about the house, each group having its own particular dealings, one in Government Stocks, another in English rail- ways, a third in Foreign securities, and so on. A broker having received an order from a customer to sell £1,000 Great Eastern Railway Stock, would go to the English railway group and inquire of a jobber the price or quotation for Great Easterns, without disclosing whether he wants to buy or to sell. The jobber replies, "115 1/4 to 115 1/2"; whereupon the broker says, "I sell at 115 1/4," when the bargain is completed, without any memorandum or written contract, the verbal communication being alone in use, and the jobber is bound by it. It will be observed that the lower price, 115 1/4, is accepted by the broker on behalf of his customer, as a sale is always effected at the lowest quotation, and a purchase at the highest. Another broker pre- sently goes to the jobber and asks the same question receiving the same reply, 115 1/4 to 115 1/2 the broker says, "I buy of you at 115 1/2," being the highest quotation. The difference of 5s. between the sale and the purchase is the Job- ber's profit. The broker charges his customer his own commission or brokerage on the trans- action, which ranges from 2s. 6d. per cent. on the Government and Colonial Stocks up to 10s. per cent. on railway stocks. This is the elementary stage of the business of the Stock Exchange, but the variety of the securities dealt in, under constantly changing circumstances, the number of transactions, and the amount of money changing hands, involve intricate accounts and arrangements, which need not be particularised here. Accounts are settled fort- nightly, the precise dates being fixed some time before by the Committee of the house.

Many speculators, however, especially those who have bought stocks and shares with the expectation that they will speedily rise in price, do not find it convenient to pay the purchase- money on the appointed settling day; so pay- ment may, by arrangement, be carried over to the next settling day. For the accommodation a certain charge, which is called "contango," is made, the amount varying with the value of money and the quality of the stock. "Back- wardation," on the other hand, is a commission paid in order to postpone the delivery of stocks or shares which a speculator contracts to sell, but which he never possessed. He is a specu- lator for the fall, hoping by the delay to be able to purchase the same stocks and shares at a less price than he bargained to sell them for, and so make a profit out of the transaction. Specu- lations for a rise are known on the Stock Exchange as "Bulls," and their object is by every manner of means to get the prices of the stocks they are dealing in pushed up as much as possible. Speculators for a fall are called "Bears," and they are equally anxious to send prices *down*. So sensitive is the stock market that prices are easily affected; the rumoured prospect of an important dividend from a rail- way company will at once probably influence the price of its shares, whilst a report of a disastrous accident will have the contrary effect. A "boom" in the money market is a cheerful desire on the part of the speculative public to be purchasers at advancing prices, and this betokens good business for the brokers and jobbers. A "boom" in any particular stock is a buoyancy in prices, caused by some favourable rumour, whether founded or unfounded, more often the latter, and set agoing in the interest of persons who desire to get rid of surplus stock. A "boom" in railway shares is often brought about by increased traffic receipts; a "boom" in mining shares is caused by one or two com- panies having produced more gold this month than last; and a "boom" in foreign stocks is due to the settlement of some political or other difficulty, &c., &c. A "slump" is just the reverse, being an unaccountable depression which sometimes fastens upon the specula- tive world, and betrays distrust in everything. Unless this feeling is checked in time it degenerates into "panic," when prices fall to a ruinously low figure.

Each fortnightly settlement includes three days — the first being continuation or "con tango" day, when all transactions of a specula- tive description are arranged to be carried over to the next settlement day. The second is the ticket day, when the names of purchasers and sellers are handed over. The third is pay-day when all amounts or balances due for stocks bought or sold are paid or received. The great bulk of business being purely speculative, the first day is the busiest; after noon on that day all new transactions entered into are for settle- ment at the next account day, unless otherwise specially arranged.

Any sums of money may be invested in, or any particular amount of stock purchased of, the Government Funds, through a broker or banker, and there is practically no limit to the quantity that may be held. In the books of the Bank of England an account is opened, and the name, address, and description of the investor care- fully registered. A memorandum is given of the transaction, but it is of value only as such, not being in the nature of a certificate or receipt, and it is not required to be given up or produced in the event of a sale or transfer of the stock or any portion of it. Accounts may be opened in one, two, three, or four names, but not more, and four different accounts may be open at the same time in the same name or names, but they must be distinguished as accounts A, B, C, and D.

In order to sell stock the holder may attend at the Bank of England himself accompanied by his broker, and then and there have the transfer made and the money paid. But this would be unusual and held to imply mistrust, without perhaps occasion for it. The safest plan is for the holder to instruct his bankers to carry out the transaction, and give them a Power of Attorney to enable them to do so. A special form of power is provided by the Bank of Eng- land, the cost of which is 11s. 6d. The Inscribed or Registered Stocks of most of the Colonial Governments are dealt with in the same way, as well as Indian stocks and the stocks of many of our larger towns. The account of an investor may be added to or diminished at any time with- out difficulty or delay.

The stocks and shares of railway and other companies may be purchased through a broker or banker, and the holder passes them over to a buyer by a formal deed of transfer. The purchaser's name, address, and description are carefully registered in the books of the company, and he has then accepted all the responsibilities that may attach to the shares. For instance, the shares he has bought may be only partly paid up. The shares in railway companies are usually paid up in full, but it may so happen in an issue of new shares that they are paid up by periodical instalments; in which case what has already been paid is known as "scrip," and retains that name until developed into fully-paid shares. A company formed of £20 shares may have called up only £5 on each, and with no intention of demanding more, yet the holder is liable for £15 on every share he holds, and before he invests his money he should be careful to ascertain the full extent of his liability. Some little time after the transfer of the stock or shares has been completed, a certificate will be issued by the company, giving full particulars of the holding, and this certificate must be care- fully preserved, as it will be required to be given up before all or any portion of the property can be sold. The Colonial, foreign, and other bonds payable to the bearer, which have been pre- viously described, are purchasable through a broker or banker, and handed over without any transfer or other formality. Bonds of this description should be left in the safe custody of a banker, who would cut off and collect the interest coupons attached, as they became due.

As an example of the hazard incurred by keeping securities of this kind in one's own house, the writer remembers a case where a gentleman was examining in a room of his house, by the light of a candle, some bonds which he afterwards locked up in an iron safe. It was dark outside and the blind was drawn up, so that any one from the garden could see all that was going on in the room. Next morning the empty safe was found in the grounds and the contents had been carried off. All the par- ticulars of the bonds were at once telegraphed to the Stock Exchange, the London banks, and the Police authorities. Some months afterwards the bonds turned up in the hands of a banker in London, who had received them from an agent abroad. An action was brought by the original owner for their recovery, but it was of no avail, as the securities had come into the hands of the banker in the course of regular business, and so the loser could get no redress and, moreover, had to pay a large amount in costs.

The broker, who is a member of the Stock Exchange, from the precautions taken on his admission, should be a responsible person, whom it would be safe to entrust with any business which might be put into his hands. His deal- ings, however, are chiefly on behalf of the bankers and outside brokers, acting for them- selves and the public. There are numerous outside brokers (that is, brokers who are not members of the Stock Exchange) in London and all over the country. In every profession there are some doubtful members, and stock- broking has its fair share, but with ordinary vigilance on the part of their customers, well- established brokers will carry out their com- missions faithfully and reasonably. As to the advice, however, a broker may have to offer in the way of investments, it must be remembered that he is no more than mortal, and would at times be prone to submit such securities as he him- self, on behalf of a client, would most desire to dispose of. In this way, too, the country broker is liable to be pressed by his London agent to get rid of particular stocks or shares which hang heavy on hand. However, bearing this well in mind, an investor may gain much useful infor- mation from his broker, although for sound advice his banker is to be preferred.

Members of the Stock Exchange are not allowed to advertise themselves or their firms, but most of the daily newspapers in London have an agent in the house, either a jobber or broker, who furnishes to his principal for publication a daily report of the state of the markets and the current prices of the day, which in that way reach the eye of the public. It may be assumed that in the better class of journals the information thus afforded is perfectly trust- worthy, although some years since one of the leading newspapers was imposed upon by its agent, who took advantage of his position to manipulate certain matters for his own ends. Less scrupulous publications, however, are freely made use of to influence the public, to cry up or prejudice the markets and particular concerns. The provincial broker, as a rule, limits his ad- vertisement to the name and address of his firm, with a quotation of the prices of a few of the stocks mostly dealt in, and monthly, or quar- terly, sends an extended list to his customers. The outside broker who advertises himself freely in the newspapers, as well as by pamphlets and circulars, is to be avoided. He will invite you to participate in his system — always an in- fallible one — of operating. He will suggest "options," "put and call," the "cover" system, and other devices by which the inexperienced may be mystified and beguiled into losing their money. However astute a man may consider himself, experience proves that, with amateurs, this kind of gambling is sure to result in loss.

An ingenious mode of practising on the cre- dulity of the public may be noticed in some financial publications. An editorial notice or subsidised paragraph will be inserted in the paper, extolling the merits and predicting the certain success of some concern which it is desired to bolster up or to foist upon the public. This is done in such a way that the reader is expected to believe that it is the genuine ex- pression of a truthful opinion by the editor, who has obtained his information from unimpeach- able sources. Of course, this peculiar kind of advertisement has to be paid for, but it has its advantages to the advertiser, for it can (for a consideration) be quoted by the country papers as unbiassed news, and attention called to it in a money article or leaderette. The pamphlets issued by the advertising outside broker are sometimes amusingly artless in the endeavour to sell shares and attract custom. On the first page will be found some paragraphs setting forth the merits and prospects of certain named companies, and advising the reader to buy shares in them without a day's delay, as a con- siderable and speedy rise in value is assured. One may be permitted to wonder why the broker and all his friends do not rush in and secure every share that is to be had. At the end of the paper the reason will be discovered; in every one of the concerns referred to shares are offered for sale, which cannot be got rid of in the regular market. It must be inferred that some credulous persons are taken in by this transparent artifice, or it would not be so con- stantly practised. The object of these publica- tions is chiefly to puff up doubtful securities, in the hope that some fatuous speculator may be tempted to buy. It is delightful when two of these gentry fall out and expose each other's knavery. The reader is assured that "Codlin's his friend, not Short"; the latter is denounced as a fraud and retaliates, but no action for libel is brought, because both know that on either side the imputation is justifiable.

It may excite surprise in some who are favoured with circulars and prospectuses which are, through the Post Office, sown broadcast over the whole country, how the name and address of a comparatively obscure individual should be known. Prospectus and circular distributing is a business conducted on a regular system. When it is desired to invite subscrip- tions to float some new company or to bolster up some concern, the share lists of the same sort of companies already in existence are drawn upon for names and addresses; and court directories also furnish a wide field for operations.

At the present time the rage appears to have set in for forming limited liability companies out of private industrial concerns or trading firms. Most of these companies, we are told by an authority, "are brought out under the same auspices" — that is they are started and floated by a skilled personage known as a "promoter." The stereotyped prospectus must now be familiar to most people, and the public respond freely to the invitation to subscribe for shares, without consideration or inquiry. The prospectus is usually replete with statistics, showing the suc- cess which has attended the business whilst in private hands, and the enormous profits made; and one is apt to wonder why they did not keep it to themselves, instead of inviting the public to share in the gains. But there are good com- panies and bad companies, and it is to be feared that the latter largely preponderate. A good company may have a genuine reason for its existence, such as the desire of a last surviving partner to retire from active life, or the growth of the business to such an extent that more capital is required than could be obtained from a private person, or upon some other equally valid ground. A bad company is often the make-shift to save a decaying firm from insol- vency, or to dispose of a business at a price quite out of proportion to its real value. The prospectus affords no opportunity of discrimi- nating what is genuine and likely to succeed from what is false and sure to fail. If, as it has been said, eighty per cent. of companies floated sooner or later go to the wall, then, indeed, inquiry and much circumspection are needed before entering upon a speculation of the kind. It must be said, however, that many companies formed from trading concerns have become well established and profitable, and if permanency could be relied upon, they furnish a field for lucrative investments. Those adventures which are unduly pressed upon the notice of the public should be regarded with suspicion. If a thing is really good in itself, it will not require much persuasion to commend itself; and if bad, no purchased laudation will make it better. A subtle mode of advertising is just now coming into vogue, which, though expensive, will for a time be successful. There need be no reflection on the companies which adopt it, though calcu- lated to beguile the innocent and confiding in- vestor. A leaf or two introduced in some of our illustrated papers, in no wise differing in the printing from the remainder of the publica- tion, and appearing as though it formed part of the regular pabulum offered to the public. This leaf or leaves contain well-executed pic- tures of the works and machinery and other interesting objects connected with the industry of a company to which it is desired to call attention, and a descriptive account is given of its magnitude and success. To the casual reader all this would appear to be a matter of public interest, offered to the public as part of the regular business of the paper, but it is only an ingenious form of advertisement and has to be paid for as such, but that is of no consequence if the effect is produced, of a rise in the price of the shares. There are some companies whose shares are quoted at such enormous premiums, and which pay such high dividends, that the investor is sorely tempted to embark in similar undertakings, apparently, that are brought be- fore the public. But these prosperous concerns are in most cases first taken up by a syndicate — that is, a certain limited number of persons behind the scenes — who finance and float the company, and when success has been attained, the public are granted the privilege of purchas- ing shares — but at such a price as the syndicate choses to put upon them, and, not seldom, that is the highest they ever attain. This is particu- larly the case with mining companies, the successful ones having certainly only benefited the few. This syndicate system has given rise to a bogus imitation, which, however, appears to have met with but limited success. Circulars in lithographed writing, marked "private and con- fidential," and implying a friendly interest in those addressed, are sent to persons whose names are obtained in the manner already indi- cated. An invitation is given them to join a syndicate about to be formed to float a certain company, the profits arising from the operation being certain and enormous. Again, if it be such an excellent and certain venture, why offer a share to an entire stranger? These circulars are very speciously worded, and there is an air of candour about them likely to allure. Anyone foolish enough to subscribe would probably, after an interval, be informed that owing to un- foreseen circumstances the adventure had turned out a failure, and that all the money had gone in expenses. Successful gold mines have yielded large fortunes to their proprietors, but it must be remembered that mines have but a limited existence, and once they are worked out the money invested in them is lost; for when they cease to yield ore there is nothing more to be obtained from them. Promiscuous dealing in mine shares is nothing more or less than gambling, or taking part in a lottery in which the blanks are overwhelming and the prizes next to nothing. If an enterprise has in it any degree of soundness or promise, there are plenty of the knowing ones ready to step in and take all the advantages to be gained; it is the des- perate ventures and unscrupulous swindles that the public are mostly pressed to support — only to lose their money. It is to be hoped that the dupes are at length awake to the pit-falls dug for them by the mining company promoter and speculator, whose seductive paragraphs are everywhere in evidence in the advertising sheets of the day.

A typical example — and not a fictitious one — of hundreds of knavish concerns foisted on the public may be quoted. A certain company, of which no prospectus has been issued, nor of which anything is publicly known, appears in the mining lists. One day, a paragraph in a financial paper reports that the agent for the mines, on the spot, has cabled that the promise of success exceeds all expectations, that samples of ore, yielding three ounces to the ton, have been found, and that the necessary machinery must be sent out at once. This is followed up by an editorial leaderette (of course, paid for), in which the writer expresses surprise that the shares of so promising an enterprise should be at so low a price, and predicting a rapid advance when the work is further developed. These notices effect their purpose to the extent of rais- ing the quotations of the shares a few shillings, but this is not enough for the promoter; a cir- cular is next issued, in the usual way, to the effect that the directors have been fortunate enough to secure additional property near their own, which furnishes wood and water, so essential to the proper development of the mine, and including, moreover, alluvial pits abounding in gold. An elaborate lithographed sketch of the property, with mines at work and a steam-engine, accom- panies the circular, and the whole presents an appearance of real business. The next move is the statutory meeting of the shareholders, which, however, is very sparsely attended, as the vic- tims are chiefly people residing in the country, who do not care to incur the expense of a journey to London. The man who presides at the meet- ing, an outside broker, begins a speech by apologising for the absence of the chairman of the company (of whom the shareholders hear for the first time), and then goes on to describe with tedious detail the technical working of the mine, the stopes and veins, and bunches of gold that there are, and the stamps, machinery, &c., that there are to be. He describes what has been done in the alluvial pits, and the prospect of wealth to be drawn therefrom as beyond the dreams of avarice, and winds up with warm con- gratulation of the proprietors on the valuable property they possess. Whether he has over- done his part or something prejudicial to the company leaks out, the shares which had changed hands at 10s. gradually drop to 5s. Then a circular goes the round in which some member of the ring of knaves invites the public to join a syndicate to buy up five thousand of these shares which he has, through peculiar circum- stances, been able to secure the refusal of at 4s. a share. A special meeting of the shareholders is next called, when it is announced that more capital is required, and that it will be necessary to pay up the one shilling per share which still remains outstanding. A last desperate effort to get rid of the shares at any price is then resorted to before the call of one shilling per share becomes payable, and some thousands are offered at one shilling and sixpence each. After the time has expired for paying the call, a last circular is issued, intimating briefly that the eminent engineer, who has originally given such a glowing account of the mine, now reports that there is no present indication of gold on the property, but that possibly some might be found if they dug deep enough!

The name of the company has disappeared from the mining share list, and it will be heard of no more. It is doubtful if there ever was any property, or engineer, or board of directors, or, in fact, anything more than the outside broker and his confederates.

Of the *bona fide* speculative undertakings in South Africa and Australia, the exploration and finance companies, or some few of them, have made the largest profits. Their system, broadly speaking, is to acquire certain tracts of land in a gold-bearing district, and then let small portions on lease to different subsidiary companies, which have been floated to develop gold or whatever else these portions may con- tain. The price paid to the parent company is made up of; perhaps, one half in cash and the other in the shares of the new concern. An im- mediate profit accrues from the payment in cash, and there is a wide field for further gains if the operations of the subsidiary companies are suc- cessful. But in this, as in all speculative enter- prises, the prizes have been few and the blanks many.

CHAPTER IX. LIFE INSURANCE.

LADIES do not take advantage of the system of life insurance to the extent one would expect, seeing the benefits it is capable of conferring upon themselves and their belongings; and as their indifference is no doubt, in many cases, owing to a want of knowledge of the subject, a chapter thereon may be useful.

Life insurance is an admirable system, devised, in all its ramifications, to provide against loss or damage through the various contingencies to which human nature is subject.

A simple life insurance is that by which a person may leave behind him a sum of money for the benefit of those who, during his life, have been dependent upon him. For example, a husband, whose income is entirely derived from his own exertions, desires to make some pro- vision for his wife and children in the event of his dying before them. At the age of thirty he may, by paying £25 a year to an Insurance Office, secure at his death, whenever it may happen, £1,000, for the benefit of his wife or chil- dren, or as he may direct by his will. In a way insurance is a kind of savings bank, but impos- ing an obligation on the part of the depositor to save a certain sum every year. In the case of the bank, the savings are optional, and cease at death; whereas by insurance, the return of a large sum is the result of the death of the com- pulsory depositor. If a person put by £25 every year and invested that sum in the Government Funds at 2 1/2 per cent., or deposited the same sum annually in a bank, at the same rate of interest, it would take him twenty-eight years to accumu- late £1,000, if he lived so long; whereas by an insurance on his life for the same amount, if he died a week after the first payment of £25 had been made, the £1,000 insured would be paid to his representatives. It might be said that if the person lived longer than the term of twenty- eight years and went on saving the £25 every year, he would in the end accumulate more than £1,000. This, however, is met by insuring in such manner that the insurance carries "profits," that is, additions made by the gains of the office from time to time. If insurance be made in this manner, for which a slightly higher rate of pre- mium is paid, it will be found that, however long a person might live, more would accrue at death by insurance than by saving.

There are in active existence so many insur- ance companies of good repute and undoubted stability that no difficulty need be experienced in making a judicious selection. Of course, the intelligent insurer would prefer an office whose system would best suit his own requirements. There are two kinds of Insurance Companies, one known as a "Mutual" office, in which *all* the profits which may be earned are periodically added to the amount insured, the other in the form of a Joint-Stock Company, in which a small proportion of the profits are distributed amongst the Shareholders and the remainder added to the Insurances. The Mutual Office dividing the whole of its profits amongst the insured would appear to be the more advantageous of the two, and undoubtedly it is, all other things being equal; but insurances may be effected which do not share in the profits, at lower rate of pre- mium, and in that case one system is as good as the other. The intending insurer would do well to obtain the prospectuses of several offices, which he can easily do by writing for them direct to the head office or by applying to the several agents of the companies who abound in all towns; and carefully compare one with another. It will be found, perhaps, that one office charges a less annual premium for an in- surance than another, but this may be compen- sated for by the latter declaring larger profits, or giving advantages in other ways. For instance, a certain "Mutual" office charges for an insur- ance of £1,000, on the death of a person begin- ning to insure at the age of thirty, a pre- mium of £26 16s. 8d. per annum, whereas a certain Joint-Stock Company's demand is only £24 14s. 3d.; but the advantages offered by the former in the shape of larger bonuses, though deferred, are greater, while the benefit of a less annual payment is of course immediate. Where the insurance is effected at the same age and for the same amount, but with no other benefit or profit prospectively than the bare amount, the premium in the former case is £21 4s. 2d., and in the latter £21

15s. 10d. There are good offices, however, where the premium charged is less than this.

There is at least one office which insures upon what is called the half-credit system. One-half the usual premium is paid for a certain term of years, and thereafter the full premium is charged. This may be useful in a case where a person wishes to insure while young and the premiums are low, and at the same time is desir- ous of deferring the full payment until his income is so improved that he can better afford it. This system is carried still further by an in- surer only paying half the premium during his lifetime, the other half being accumulated until his death, and then, with interest added, de- ducted from the amount payable in respect of the insurance policy.

Having chosen the insurance office or com- pany which best suits his purpose, the proposer applies to its nearest agent and makes known his desire to insure his life. A form containing printed queries somewhat like the following (though offices differ somewhat in details) will be placed before him and the blank spaces filled in either by the agent or himself.

———————- | PROPOSAL   FOR   LIFE   ASSURANCE | |

————-| | | Full   Name

_____ | | |

Profession or Occupation _____ ||

1.   Life   proposed   to   be   Assured | Business   Address

_____ | | | Residence

_____ | | |

Married or Single _____ |

|

_____

_____| | 2.
Age next Birthday _____ years. Born at

_____ | |
on the _____ day of _____ in the
year 18_____ | | (Evidence to be produced.) | |

_____

_____| | 3. Has
he resided out of Europe? | | | If so, where, and for what period? | | |

_____

_____| | 4. Is
he, and has he always been, of sober and | | | temperate habits? | | |

_____

_____| | 5. Has
he had any serious illness or disease | | | tending to shorten life? | | |

_____

_____| | 6. Has
any near relative died of any hereditary| | | disease? | | |

_____

_____| | 7. (1)
Has a proposal to effect an Assurance on| | | his life ever been declined?
|_____

_____| | (2) Or accepted at more than the ordinary | | | rate?
|_____

_____| | (3) If so, on how many occasions, and | | | when, and by what office
or offices? | | |

_____

_____| | 8. Is

there any other circumstance which ought | | | to be communicated in order to enable the | | | Company to judge fairly of the risk? | | |

———| |If the |

Name

——— |

|person has 9. (1) Who is his usual Medical Attendant? | Residence

—— | |never |

Has known him _____ years. | |required (2) When was he last in professional atten- | Date of Attendance

————————————————————————————————————— | |Medical | Ailment

————————————————————————————————— |

|attendance,

———

———| |the

fact | 1st Friend. | 2nd Friend. | |should be | | (if necessary: see marginal note to | |stated, and 10. Mention an intimate friend, who is not in- | | Question.) |

|reference terested in this Assurance, to be referred | Name

_____ | _____ |

|given to to for information as to health and habits | Residence

_____ | _____ | |TWO

friends, of life | Profession or | | |in answer to | Occupation _____ |

_____ | |Question 10. | Has known

him _____ years | Has known him _____ years. | |

———

———| |If the |

Name

—— |

|Proposal be 11. Name, &c., of the person in whose favour | Profession or

Occupation _____ | |upon the the

Assurance is to be effected? Business Address
_____ | |person's own |

Residence

_____ | |life

these

_____

_____|

|enquiries 12. Is the pecuniary interest in the Life to be | | |need not be Assured, which is the object of this | | |answered. Assurance, to the full amount thereof? | | |

_____

_____

————————-| | Sum to be Assured £_____ With or without Profits? _____ | | Is the Policy to be for Life? _____ Are the premiums to be payable Yearly? _____ | | I do hereby declare that the above statements are true, and that this Proposal and Declaration shall be the basis of | | the contract for effecting the above-mentioned Assurance, which Assurance is also conditional on the accuracy, in all | | respects, of the statement for the Medial Officer, made, or to be made, by the person whose life is proposed for Assurance. | | Date _____ Signature of the Person in | |

whose favour the Assur-

_____ | | Witness

_____ ance is to be effected. | | Address

and Occupation _____ |

_____

_____

————————-

The proposer has now to undergo one other formality, disagreeable no doubt, but absolutely necessary, and that is the medical examination. This is done by the medical officer of the com- pany who has to certify that the proposer is free from any defect likely to shorten his natural life, and that he is sound "in wind and limb." Defi- ciency in the number of the latter is, however, not considered unsoundness, as a person with one arm, or one leg, or one eye may be just as good a "life" and therefore equally eligible for insurance with him who is perfect. All the en- quiries in the form are made by the Office and the expenses (including the doctor's fee) paid by the Company.

If the proposal is accepted, the proposer is informed of the fact and then pays his first pre- mium in advance, it may be a year's, or half-a- year's, or a quarter year's, at his own option, and he then becomes (subject to the rules of the particular company) the insured.

A few days subsequently a life policy will be sent to the insured. This is a document setting forth, in full, the terms of the agreement between the Company and the insured, and must be care- fully kept, in such wise that it may readily be discovered by the person for whose benefit it is ultimately intended. The writer once found amongst some old papers a life policy in the name of a man who had been dead for many years. On enquiry at the office it was found that the amount which was payable at his death had, by some neglect, never been claimed. The company of course at once paid the money, and a needy sister was very much benefited.

Thirty days' grace are usually allowed for subsequent payments of premium. It is custo- mary for insurance offices to forward to each policy holder a reminder, from one to four weeks before the periodical payments for premium become due, but the absence of any such notice will not be accepted as an excuse for non-pay- ment, and if the premium be not paid before the thirty days' grace allowed have expired, the policy becomes void. It may, however, be re- vived upon paying a fine and producing a medical certificate of health.

Should the proposal be declined the fact will be notified to the proposer, but he will not be informed of the reason. Proposals are rejected because of something wrong being discovered by the medical examiner, or because of intemperate habits, or that the history of his near relations in regard to health and longevity is unfavour- able; anything in short that indicated that the proposer will not, in all probability, live as long as a healthy man is expected to live is enough reason for declining to insure his life.

Insurances may be effected for a limited period, say for one, three, or five years, at about one half the premium charged for the whole term of life. If the insured dies within the period, the amount of the policy is paid, but the insurance ends with the periods of time agreed upon. This class of insurance is useful in many ways. For example: A person with a certain income for life is desir- ous of borrowing £500, to be repaid by annual instalments. There would be no difficulty in finding a lender, provided he could be sure of repayment; and this could be secured in this manner — the borrower would assign to the lender £100 a year of income for five years for the gra- dual discharge of the loan; the borrower's life would also be insured for five years and the Policy assigned to the lender. If the borrower lived for five years the loan would be paid out of the income. In the event of his death, it would be paid by means of the insurance money.

Another example: a child aged seventeen is entitled to a fortune, large or small, at the age of twenty-one, but meanwhile is wholly depen- dent on its mother who has only an annuity for her life. Should the mother die before the child becomes of age the latter would be left without the means of subsistence. In such a case the prudent mother would insure her own life for the four years which must elapse before the child could come into the fortune, for such a sum as would keep it from want, so that in case the mother died the insurance money would provide the means of living. The premium charged on this class of insurance is moderate; about £2 6s. for a person aged fifty; and the outlay by the mother could be subsequently repaid when the child was in a position to do so.

There are other special modes of insurance to prevent loss or damage in cases of remote risk; indeed almost any chance of loss through the possibility of something improbable occurring may be guarded against by insurance. For instance, a lady aged forty-five has been married for twenty years and has had no children. If she has a son her property will descend to him; if she dies childless it passes to a nephew. The chance of the lady having a son is extremely remote but still there is a possibility, and it is against loss by this possibility happening that the nephew takes out a policy of insurance for any reasonable amount, the premium charged being surprisingly small and payable in one sum down.

BONUSES.

It has been mentioned in a previous page that insurance has the advantage over the savings bank, no matter how long a person may live, and this is brought about by the operation of Bonuses, so called. These are the whole pro- fits in the case of a Mutual Company, and the larger proportion of the profits in the case of a Joint-Stock Company, which are distributed amongst the policy holders. At the end of every five years, in some cases seven, a valuation is made of all the property of the Company and on the other hand is ascertained what the company is liable for, present and prospective. The difference between the two constitutes the sur- plus or profits, assuming of course that the assets preponderate. This seems at first sight to be a very simple process, but in reality the most intricate calculations are necessary to arrive at mathematical accuracy; but this needs no further notice here. The bonus being declared, it may be dealt with in various ways.

1. — It may be added to the amount insured, and so payable at death.
2. — It may be commuted for an immediate payment in cash. (In this case the amount will, of course, be less than in No. 1.)
3. — It may be applied in a permanent reduction of the future annual premiums, or a proportionately larger reduction of these for the next five or seven years, and in other ways. Most offices granting every reasonable facility for applying profits in any way the insured may consider desirable.

Endowment Insurance. — This is a class of insurance by which an insurer may receive the amount of a policy himself during his life, at an age to be fixed at the time the insurance is effected. Should he die before reaching the age specified, the money is payable to his represen- tatives.

It may also be so arranged that instead of receiving the money at a certain age, he may be paid a fixed sum annually for the rest of his life thereafter.

For example — a person at the age of thirty may insure £1,000 to be paid to him on attain- ing the age of sixty. The annual premiums for insurances of this kind vary with different offices; but they can be effected at the age named, at about £28 10s. for the £1,000. If the person died before attaining the specified age, the money would be paid to his representatives; if he sur- vived, he could either receive the £1,000, or be granted an annuity for the remainder of his life of £92 a year. In the case of females the annuity would be £83 only, as they are supposed to live longer than males.

Non-forfeitable Policies. — This plan provides for the continuance of insurance upon the life of a policy holder should the insured from any cause be unable to keep up his premiums. The prin- ciple of this scheme ensures that, in considera- tion of the premiums already paid, a policy for a certain amount — less of course than that named in the original policy, which would be cancelled — would be granted freed from all future pay- ments in respect of premiums, and the insurance money of the new policy would be payable at death. For example — a person insures his life for £1,000 at the age of thirty, the annual pre- mium on which would be £25 a year. At the age of forty he finds himself unable any longer to pay the annual premium, but to avoid the loss of the £250 which he has paid during the ten years, he will surrender the old policy for £1,000 and will be granted a new one, say for half the amount, payable at death, and he will not be called upon to pay any further premiums.

Settlement Policies. — This class of policy is issued under the Married Women's Property Act (1882), whereby a trust can be created for the benefit of a wife or children of an insured person, the trustee being the Insurance Com- pany. The advantage of this is that such a policy does not constitute a part of the husband's estate or become subject to his debts, either whilst living or at his death, so that in the latter event the money is paid to the widow or children direct for their own use. A policy of this kind, if necessity should arise, could also be exchanged for a non-forfeitable policy in the manner before pointed out.

Endowments for Children. — A parent, by paying a premium of about £5 5s. annually, can secure to a child aged six a sum of £100, on its attain- ing the age of twenty-one. Should the child die before reaching that age, the money paid in pre- miums is not lost, for it is all returned to the parent without deduction.

By this means a marriage portion or outfit for a girl, or a start in business for a boy can be provided to any amount that may be desired.

Insurance on Joint Lives is another mode of insurance, very useful in particular cases. For example: a mother aged fifty has an income, for her life and no longer, of £300 a year, and she has a daughter aged twenty, who has no means of her own, present or prospective, being entirely dependent on her mother. The joint lives are insured for, say, £2,000, which would cost in premium £100 a year; the insurance money to be paid at the death of the first of the two. If the daughter died first the mother would get back, by the insurance money, possibly more than she had paid in premiums. If the mother died first, say at the age of seventy, by that time the daughter would have attained the age of forty, and the £2,000 would be paid to her. With the money she might, if she so pleased, buy an annuity for life of £110 a year.

Insurance on the Longest of Two Lives, payable on the death of the survivor, is useful in cases where land or house property is held on lease, so that there may be no pecuniary loss when the lease expires. The rate of premium is in this case naturally less than where the insurance is to be paid on the earlier of the two deaths.

SURRENDERS.

If from any cause it is desired to give up a policy and discontinue paying any more pre- miums, the offices will pay to the insured what is called the surrender value of the policy, at the same time cancelling it and all its conditions. This surrender value may be roughly calculated at about 40 per cent. of the premiums paid, in a case were bonuses have been added to a policy, and about 33 per cent. of the premiums paid in a case where the bonuses have not been so applied. For example: a person has paid £25 a year in premiums for ten years — in all £250 — on a policy for £1,000, to which has been added £60 in the shape of bonuses. The surrender value in such a case would be £100. But if the insured had taken his bonuses in cash, or his policy did not carry profits, then the surrender value would be £82 10s. only.

Any insurance office will lend the insured, on the security of the policy, an amount of money not exceeding the surrender value, and the rate of interest is usually moderate.

In this case there would be no necessity to abandon the policy, which would be kept alive and increased by added bonuses as before.

FIRE INSURANCE.

This is a distinct branch of insurance business, the object being to compensate a person in case of pecuniary loss through the accidental burning of his property. By paying annually a com- paratively small amount in the shape of pre- mium, a person may insure that in case of the destruction by fire of such of his goods as may be specified in a fire policy, issued by the Insur- ance Company, he will be recouped their value. Nearly all the Fire Insurance offices are agreed in charging a certain rate of premium, which is called the tariff rate. For dwelling-houses built of brick or stone with slate or tile roof, the rate is only 1s. 6d. for every £100. For more hazard- ous buildings such as thatched houses, ware- houses, inns, shops, &c., the rates are higher, according to the nature of the risk. Household furniture and the other contents of a brick or stone house can be insured at various rates, or they may be included in one insurance with the house, when the rate would be 2s. per cent. for the whole.

It should be remembered that there is a limit, usually of 5 per cent., of the whole sum so in- sured, placed on any one work of art which may be destroyed.

For instance, a picture valued at £200 maybe burnt in a house which, with the contents, is insured for £2,000 If the picture were alone destroyed, the office would only compensate to the extent of £100, being 5 per cent. on the £2,000, the total amount of the insurance. Any particular picture or work of art may, however, be specially insured by itself.

Insurances should never be made for a greater sum than the value of the property insured, as it would be paying more premium for no purpose. The offices take good care that they pay no more than the actual value of the property destroyed, which they have the means of ascertaining with some degree of accuracy.

It has been found necessary to subject the insurance of farming stock to special conditions. A farmer having stock of the value, say, of £1,000, might reason in this way: "My ricks, implements, crops, &c., are situated widely apart, and it is difficult to imagine that all could be consumed in one and the same fire; therefore, I will insure the whole stock for £500 only, then I shall have to pay only half the amount in the premium I should be liable for in case I insured to the full value." The offices are, however, quite alive to this kind of reasoning, and frustrate the intention by inserting what is called the "average" clause in the policy, the effect of which is that in the event of a claim being made for loss by fire, only one half of the value would be made because only one half of the value of the stock was insured. Live stock, however, may be separately insured without the average clause, and animals killed by lightning are paid for if insured against loss by fire.

There are other offices which insure against loss by special contingencies, such as damage to glass houses, and cattle, and garden produce, by hailstorms; destruction of boilers by explosion, of plate glass, and from accident or disease affecting cattle. There are companies, too, which insure against accidents sustained by rail, road, or water, guaranteeing a specified sum in case of death, and compensation in case of injury. Also societies which take the place of sureties and guarantee an insurer against loss or default by anyone in his employ; and companies which undertake to make good any loss arising from burglary or larceny. In all cases, of course, the liability of the office is limited to a certain declared amount.

CHAPTER X. BUILDING SOCIETIES.

THE main object of a Building Society is to aid a man to become proprietor of his own dwelling. This can be accomplished by means of the society in two different ways:- 1, by depositing with the society periodical money savings until, with the interest allowed, enough has been accumu- lated to buy a house; 2, by borrowing from the society a sufficient sum to purchase a house and repaying the loan, with interest, by instal- ments spread over a term of years. A person desiring to become a depositor must qualify for membership of the society by paying an entrance fee of; say, 2s. 6d. He then takes up a share and, by paying periodical instalments according to the tables, he becomes entitled at the end of the appointed time to receive £100.

The same applies proportionately to a half share of £50 or to a quarter share of £25. For example, as regards the whole share, a person paying 13s. a month regularly to the society is entitled, at the end of ten years, to be repaid a lump sum of £100, and any bonus added thereto which the profits of the society may afford. If the term be fifteen years, then, to secure £100, he will have to pay only 7s. 7d. every month, and if twenty-one years, then a monthly payment of 4s. 7d. The terms vary in different societies, but those quoted have been adopted by an exist- ing institution of repute. If the term of ten years is selected, the depositor will have saved and paid to the society (with added interest) £78 in all; if the term of fifteen years is chosen he will have paid £68 5s. in all; and if twenty-one years be adopted, £57 15s. In either case, at the end of the term he has selected, the depositor will be paid back £100. Thus any one taking a share for £100, and keeping up the instalments for twenty-one years, will in the end have paid only £57 15s. for it — the difference being met by the interest paid by borrowers from the society. The following table shows particulars of other terms and the monthly subscription payable:-

Term (Years)	Monthly Subscription for a £100 share.			Term (Years)	Monthly Subscription for a £100 share.		
	£	s.	d.		£	s.	d.
3	2	12	10	13	0	9	1
4	1	18	8	14	0	8	4
5	1	10	2	15	0	7	7
6	1	4	6	16	0	6	11
7	1	0	6	17	0	6	4
8	0	17	6	18	0	5	10
9	0	15	2	19	0	5	4
10	0	13	0	20	0	5	0
11	0	11	8	21	0	4	7
12	0	10	6				

After the first year a depositor may, if desirous, withdraw, on giving one month's notice, the full amount he has paid, with interest, to the date when the subscription ceases. This prevents the possibility of any loss arising to a depositor in the event of his being unable to keep up his instalments, or desiring from any cause to with- draw from the society. It may, however, in case of a loss of confidence, operate seriously against the society, by the sudden withdrawal of de- posits. The following table shows the amount that could be claimed, in respect of the monthly subscriptions paid, at the end of the several years of membership.

SHOWING THE AMOUNT WITHDRAWABLE AT THE END OF EACH YEAR FOR THE RESPECTIVE MONTHLY SUBSCRIPTIONS STATED IN THE ABOVE TABLE.

At the end of Year of Membership	2 12 10 per month, 3 years.	1 18 8 per month, 4 years.	1 10 2 per month, 5 years.	1 4 6 per month, 6 years.	1 0 6 per month, 7 years.	17s. 6d. per month, 8 years.	15s. 2d. per month, 9 years.	13s. per month, 10 years.	11s. 8d. per month, 11 years.	10s. 6d. per month, 12 years.
	£ s. d.	£ s. d.	£ s. d.	£ s. d.	£ s. d.	£ s. d.	£ s. d.	£ s. d.	£ s. d.	£ s. d.
1st	31 14 0	23 4 0	18 2 0	14 14 0	12 6 0	10 10 0	9 2 0	7 16 0	7 0 0	6 6 0
2nd	64 19 0	47 11 0	37 2 0	30 2 8	25 4 2	21 10 6	18 13 1	15 19 9	14 7 0	12 18 3
3rd	100 0 0	73 2 0	57 1 2	46 6 10	38 15 6	33 2 0	28 13 9	24 11 9	22 1 4	19 17 2
4th	—	100 0 0	78 0 2	63 7 2	53 0 2	45 5 1	39 4 5	33 12 4	30 3 5	27 3 0
5th	—	—	100 0 0	81 4 6	67 19 2	58 0 4	50 5 8	43 1 11	38 13 7	34 16 2
6th	—	—	—	100 0 0	83 13 2	71 8 4	61 17 11	53 1 1	47 12 3	42 17 0
7th	—	—	—	—	100 0 0	85 9 9	74 1 10	63 10 1	56 19 10	51 5 10
8th	—	—	—	—	—	100 0 0	86 17 11	74 9 7	66 16 10	60 3 1
9th	—	—	—	—	—	—	100 0 0	86 0 1	77 3 8	69 9 3
10th	—	—	—	—	—	—	—	100 0 0	88 0 10	79 4 9
11th	—	—	—	—	—	—	—	—	100 0 0	89 9 11
12th	—	—	—	—	—	—	—	—	—	100 0 0
13th	—	—	—	—	—	—	—	—	—	—
14th	—	—	—	—	—	—	—	—	—	—
15th	—	—	—	—	—	—	—	—	—	—
16th	—	—	—	—	—	—	—	—	—	—
17th	—	—	—	—	—	—	—	—	—	—
18th	—	—	—	—	—	—	—	—	—	—
19th	—	—	—	—	—					

| — | — | — | — | — | | 20th | — | — | — | — | — | — | — | — | — | — |
21st | — | — | — | — | — | — | — | — | — |

At the end of Year of Membership.	9s. 1d. per month, 13 years.			8s. 4d. per month, 14 years.			7s. 7d. per month, 15 years.			6s. 11d. per month, 16 years.			6s. 4d. per month, 17 years.			5s. 10d. per month, 18 years.			5s. 4d. per month, 19 years.			5s. per month, 20 years.			4s. 7d. per month, 21 years.		
	£	s.	d.	£	s.	d.	£	s.	d.	£	s.	d.	£	s.	d.	£	s.	d.	£	s.	d.	£	s.	d.	£	s.	d.
1st	5	9	0	5	0	0	4	11	0	4	3	0	3	16	0	3	10	0	3	4	0	3	0	0	2	15	0
2nd	11	3	5	10	5	0	9	6	5	8	10	2	7	15	10	7	3	5	6	11	3	6	3	0	5	12	9
3rd	17	3	8	15	15	2	14	6	8	13	1	5	11	19	7	11	0	5	10	1	9	9	9	1	8	13	5
4th	23	9	9	21	11	0	19	11	10	17	17	5	16	7	7	15	1	5	13	15	10	12	18	7	11	17	1
5th	30	2	3	27	12	6	25	2	3	22	18	3	20	19	11	19	6	5	17	13	8	16	11	6	15	3	11
6th	37	1	5	34	0	3	30	18	3	28	4	0	25	16	11	23	15	8	21	15	4	20	8	1	18	14	1
7th	45	4	2	40	14	2	37	0	0	33	15	3	30	18	9	28	9	3	26	1	1	24	8	6	22	7	10
8th	53	18	9	49	8	3	44	18	0	40	19	10	36	5	8	33	7	8	30	11	1	28	12	11	26	5	2
9th	62	2	4	56	17	8	51	13	10	47	3	8	43	3	5	39	14	10	35	5	8	34	2	7	30	6	5
10th	70	13	5	64	14	6	58	16	5	53	13	8	49	2	7	45	4	5	41	7	5	38	16	8	34	11	9
11th	79	13	1	72	19	4	66	6	3	60	10	3	55	7	9	50	19	8	46	12	10	43	15	7	40	1	5
12th	89	1	9	81	12	4	74	3	5	67	13	8	61	19	1	57	0	5	52	3	5	48	19	5	44	16	5
13th	100	0	0	90	16	8	82	8	5	75	4	2	68	17	0	63	7	5	57	19	7	54	10	0	49	16	3
14th	—			100	0	0	91	1	9	83	2	5	76	1	10	70	0	8	64	1	6	60	0	0	55	1	1
15th	—			—			100	0	0	91	8	5	83	13	11	77	0	___	70	9	7	65	18	8	60	11	1
16th	—			—			—																				

|100 0 0 | 91 8 5 | 84 7 8 | 77 4 0 | 72 3 5 | 66 6 8 | | 17th | — | — | — | —
|100 0 0 | 92 1 10 | 84 5 3 | 78 14 5 | 72 8 0 | | 18th | — | — | — | — | — |100
0 0 | 91 13 6 | 85 11 11 | 78 15 5 | | 19th | — | — | — | — | — | — |100 0 0 |
92 16 4 | 85 9 2 | | 20th | — | — | — | — | — | — | — |100 0 0 | 92 9 8 | | 21st
| — | — | — | — | — | — | — | — |100 0 0 |

For example, the depositor of 13s. a month for a ten years' term, if he desired to withdraw his savings at the end of six years, would be entitled to £53 1s. 1d.; the depositor of 7s. 7d. a month for fifteen years could claim, at the end of the ninth year, £51 13s. 10d.; and the depositor of 4s. 7d. a month for twenty-one years could get back £44 16s. 5d. at the expiration of the twelfth year. In each case the earnings of the depositor would have been increased by the interest added.

BORROWERS.

A member desiring to effect an immediate purchase of a house or property may borrow the money required by depositing the title deeds with the society as security, and repaying the loan by instalments, monthly or quarterly. Or if he elect to build a house himself; he deposits the deeds of the land with the society and takes up a loan by instalments as the work proceeds. In this case an architect or surveyor would have to give a certificate from time to time to the effect that so much money could be advanced upon the work actually done; and the repayment of the loan would only begin when the house was finished. The following table shows the repayments required, including interest for each £100 advanced:-

| | | Term of years. |
| Monthly. | Quarterly. | |

| £ s. d. | £ s. d. || 1 | 8 14 0 | 26 4 6 || 2 | 4 10 0 | 13 11 4 || 3 | 3 3 0 | 9 9 11 |
| 4 | 2 8 9 | 7 7 0 || 5 | 2 0 3 | 6 1 4 || 6 | 1 14 7 | 5 4 3 || 7 | 1 10 6 | 4 12 0 ||
8 | 1 7 6 | 4 2 11 || 9 | 1 5 2 | 3 15 11 || 10 | 1 3 5 | 3 10 7 || 11 | 1 1 11 | 3 6
1 || 12 | 1 0 8 | 3 2 4 || 13 | 0 19 8 | 2 19 4 || 14 | 0 18 9 | 2 16 6 || 15 | 0 18 0
| 2 14 3 || 16 | 0 17 4 | 2 12 3 || 17 | 0 16 9 | 2 10 6 || 18 | 0 16 2 | 2 8 9 || 19
| 0 15 8 | 2 7 3 || 20 | 0 15 3 | 2 6 0 || 21 | 0 14 11 | 2 5 0 |

And in like proportion for larger or smaller loans.

In many societies it is a common practice to ballot amongst the members for the right to receive an advance (sometimes without carrying interest) which right may be transferred, for a consideration, to some other member.

By this table it will be seen that a person borrowing £100 for ten years would have to repay the amount by monthly instalments of £1 3s. 5d., or by quarterly instalments of £3 10s. 7d., and if borrowing for a term of twenty-one years, then by monthly instalments of 14s. 11d., or quarterly of £2 5s.

Now, if we refer to the depositor's table of rates, we shall find that he has, for a ten years' term, paid to the society £78, and received back £100; thus receiving from the society £22 (the difference) for the use of the money, plus the interest added. On the other hand, a borrower of £100 for the same term pays back, beyond the capital sum of £100, as much as £40 2s. in interest. Thus there is a difference of £18 2s. between the interest received by the depositor and that paid by the borrower. This constitutes the gross gain of the society on these trans- actions, but out of it has to be paid the expenses of the office, salaries of officials, and a reserve provided for bad debts, &c.

The social and moral utility of societies estab- lished for the direct purpose of aiding a man to become proprietor of his dwelling-house is obvious, and the above calculations seem to show that a society conducted on the plan represented would earn an ample margin of profit for all contingencies.

Doubtless the greater number of the existing building societies, including the one whose figures have been quoted, are conducted in a safe and legitimate manner, but there have been, and may still be, exceptions.

As an inducement to join a building society, people are told that they have to pay, on the instalment system, the same as though they paid the rent of a house, and in a few years will become the owner. A man who has paid for three or four years only what he would have paid for rent, would have very little hesitation in throwing up his contract with the society, if the locality became objectionable to him or the in- evitable repairs of a cheap house were more than he could bear. The money borrowed is lent chiefly upon the security of small suburban houses, a kind of property always in course of depreciation, and it may be that the society would have returned upon its hands a number of houses in a bad state of repair and in a dete- riorating locality. The instalments having ceased and the houses void, the property becomes a profitless burden upon the society and a probable ultimate loss. When "jerry" builders are large customers of a building society and have some influence, direct or indirect, with its Board of Directors, the evil is greatly aggravated. Whole streets are built with borrowed money, on specu- lation until, perhaps, there are twice as many houses as can possibly be let.

The society, to protect itself, is bound to con- tinue advancing until it is drawn completely into the net and finds itself encumbered with a lot of unsaleable and useless property. To stave off the evil day when all things must be disclosed to the trusting member, "financing" is restored to, money raised on direct deposit, and advances obtained from banks. The money thus raised tides the society over their difficulties for a time, but it may be that some rumour or report influ- ences members and depositors to withdraw their money, and eventually the coffers are empty and the end arrives.

Unhappily, in the collapse of more than one building society during the last few years there have been revealed frauds and dishonesty of the most flagrant character, and hundreds of trusting investors of the industrial classes have been ruined through the machinations of scoundrels, some of whom posed as philanthropists and ultra righteous members of society. To protect the interests of members and depositors, only men of unimpeachable character and business ability should be elected Directors of a building society, and the audit ought to be of the strictest char- acter. The balance-sheet should present details of the securities upon which the advances are made, and the auditors should certify that they have examined the deeds and identified them as representing the property described in the balance-sheet. Generally speaking, the auditors appointed by the members are not lawyers, and have not the necessary skill for verifying the documents relating to the property, indeed they are not expected to do so. One of the auditors should certainly be legally qualified to ascertain that the securities of the society do represent the properties set forth in the balance-sheet, and he should give a certificate to that effect. If this course were insisted upon, such scandals as have been brought to light could hardly be repeated, where one set of deeds was made to do duty for the assets of three distinct societies, each man- aged by the same Board of Directors; and the case in which the deeds of abandoned or destroyed property were palmed off upon the auditors to represent securities which had practically no existence. The industrial classes are less careful than those above them in seeing to the safety of their investments, and some legislation seems to be called for to prevent their hard-earned savings being frittered away by bad management or rank dishonesty.

CHAPTER XI. THE POST OFFICE SAVINGS BANK.

THIS institution offers a most admirable, con- venient, and secure depository for the savings of the industrial classes and of others. Its value to the thrifty and timid investor is incalculable, for here he may rest satisfied that he has abso- lute security, and the system is so hedged about with safeguards that it is difficult to discover any means by which loss can be sustained. The interest allowed is not high, but reasonable enough when the perfect security and the facili- ties offered are taken into consideration.

Money may be deposited by any person over seven years of age, and by anyone on behalf of children under seven. Also by married women, and with this advantage, that such deposits, unless and until the contrary is proved, are deemed to be the property of such married woman; moreover, the fact that any deposit is standing in the name of a married woman being *prima facie* evidence that she is entitled to draw the same without the consent of her husband.

Deposits may be made by two or more per- sons, provided no one of them has any other account in a Savings Bank, and by one person as trustee for another person. On opening an account a person has to sign a declaration to the effect that he takes no personal benefit from any other account in the Post Office Savings Bank or in a Trustee Savings Bank, and should this declaration not be true all sums so deposited will be liable to forfeiture.

Any person opening an account, that is, de- positing money with a Post Office Savings Bank, will receive a book in which the amount is entered, and the signature of the Postmaster and stamp of the office affixed to the entry. In addition to this he will receive from the depart- ment in London, a few days after, a receipt for the amount. Once in each year, on the anniversary of the day on which his first deposit was made, the depositor should forward his book to the Controller of Savings Banks, London, in order that it may be compared with the books of the department in London, and that the in- terest may be inserted in it. A depositor may add to his deposits at, and withdraw the whole or any part of them from, any Post Office in the United Kingdom without change of deposit- book. It will thus be obvious that all deposit accounts, although operated upon through the branch post office, are really kept at the Savings Bank Department in London, and depositors are so kept in touch with the department that complete protection is afforded them.

Any sum from one shilling upwards (but excluding pence) may be deposited, subject to certain limits. These limits are £50 a year, that is, no more than £50 will be received on deposit in any one year, but any withdrawals during the year may be re-deposited once, and once only. No more than £200 in all can be held on behalf of a depositor. The reason for these limits apparently is that the bank was created for the encouragement of saving habits in, and providing a secure place for, the money of thrifty people of small means, and not for investment of the capital of the wealthy. Interest at £2 10s. per cent. per annum, which is at the rate of sixpence a year, or one halfpenny a month, for each com- plete pound, is allowed on ordinary deposits and added to the principal; but when, by the addi- tion of interest or from any other cause, the deposit is raised to above £200, interest is allowed on £200 only, and the excess over that sum, when it amounts to £5, is applied to the purchase of Government Stock, unless the de- positor desires otherwise. When a person has £200 to the credit of his deposit account, he cannot make any further addition thereto, but the Post Office will invest this sum, or any part of it, for the depositor in Government Stock, and he can then continue paying in money to his account as before until the sum again reaches £200. No more than £200 Government Stock can be purchased in any one year, and the total amount of stock standing in a depositor's ac- count at any one time must not exceed £500. The dividends or interest on any Government Stock is credited periodically to the holder's ordinary deposit account. When a depositor wishes to withdraw the whole or any part of his money, he has to fill up and forward to the Savings Bank Department in London, a notice of withdrawal, and a form for the purpose may be obtained at any Post Office Savings Bank. He will then receive by post a warrant, on pre- sentation of which, at any branch Post Office he may have selected, payment will be made. Pay- ment by a warrant may be made to another person on behalf of the depositor, provided the latter signs a form of authority for the purpose, which form may be obtained at any Post Office Savings Bank.

A depositor of the age of sixteen and upwards may nominate any person to receive any sum (not exceeding £100) due to such depositor at his death. Every nomination must be in writing on the proper form, which may be obtained from the Controller of the Savings Bank Department, in London, to whom the nomination must be sent during the depositor's life-time.

Where, at the time of the depositor's death, the amount standing to his credit exceeds £100, it will be necessary, in order to obtain payment, that probate of his will, if any, or letters of administration (if he has died intestate), should be obtained in the usual manner.

Where the whole amount standing to the credit of a depositor at the time of his death, inclusive of Government Stock, does not exceed £100, in default of a nomination, or probate, or letters of administration, payment may be made:-

To any person who has paid the funeral expenses of the depositor;
To creditors of the depositor;
To the widow or widower of the depositor;

To the persons entitled to the effects of the deceased according to the Statute of Distribution.

To any other person establishing, to the satisfaction of the Postmaster General, a claim in accordance with the Statutes and Regulations relating to the Post Office Savings Bank.

The salient points of the Post Office Savings Bank have been placed before the reader, but in connection with the system there is another organization, for the purpose of purchasing Government Annuities and effecting Life Insur- ance, of so varied and elaborate a character that every possible requirement seems to be provided for. The "Post Office Guide," which is pub- lished quarterly, contains voluminous tables and explanations in respect of this organization, and full details and clear directions for the guidance of the public in regard to the Savings Bank.

The growing success which attends these several institutions is an unmistakable indica- tion of the value set upon them by the people. The prudent and thrifty have not been slow to take advantage of the benefits they offer, not the least of which are the freedom from doubt and anxiety they enjoy as to the safety of their money, and the certainty felt that, though other concerns may fall and involve their victims in ruin, here there is absolute and permanent security.

www.ingramcontent.com/pod-product-compliance
Lightning Source LLC
Chambersburg PA
CBHW081745200326
41597CB00024B/4396